T0320659

MACHINE LEARNING OF ROBOT ASSEMBLY PLANS

THE KLUWER INTERNATIONAL SERIES
IN ENGINEERING AND COMPUTER SCIENCE

KNOWLEDGE REPRESENTATION,
LEARNING AND EXPERT SYSTEMS

Consulting Editor

Tom Mitchell
Carnegie Mellon University

MACHINE LEARNING OF ROBOT ASSEMBLY PLANS

by

Alberto Maria Segre
Cornell University

KLUWER ACADEMIC PUBLISHERS
Boston/Dordrecht/Lancaster

Distributors for North America:
Kluwer Academic Publishers
101 Philip Drive
Assinippi Park
Norwell, Massachusetts 02061, USA

Distributors for the UK and Ireland:
Kluwer Academic Publishers
Falcon House, Queen Square
Lancaster LA1 1RN, UNITED KINGDOM

Distributors for all other countries:
Kluwer Academic Publishers Group
Distribution Centre
Post Office Box 322
3300 AH Dordrecht, THE NETHERLANDS

Library of Congress Cataloging-in-Publication Data

Segre, Alberto Maria.
  Machine learning of robot assembly plans / by Alberto Maria Segre.
    p. cm. — (Kluwer international series in engineering and
computer science. Knowledge representation, learning, and expert
systems)
  Bibliography: p.
  Includes index.
  ISBN 0-89838-269-6 : $45.00 (est.)
  1. Robotics. 2. Robots, Industrial. I. Title. II. Series.
TJ211.S43   1988   88-2652
670.42 '7—dc19   CIP

Printed in the United States of America

Table of Contents

Preface

The study of *artificial intelligence* (AI) is indeed a strange pursuit. Unlike most other disciplines, few AI researchers even agree on a mutually acceptable definition of their chosen field of study. Some see AI as a subfield of computer science, others see AI as a computationally oriented branch of psychology or linguistics, while still others see it as a bag of tricks to be applied to an entire spectrum of diverse domains.

This lack of unified purpose among the AI community makes this a very exciting time for AI research: new and diverse projects are springing up literally every day. As one might imagine, however, this diversity also leads to genuine difficulties in assessing the significance and validity of AI research. These difficulties are an indication that AI has not yet matured as a science: it is still at the point where people are attempting to lay down (hopefully sound) foundations.

Ritchie and Hanna [1] posit the following categorization as an aid in assessing the validity of an AI research endeavor:

(1)   The project could introduce, in outline, a novel (or partly novel) idea or set of ideas.

(2)   The project could elaborate the details of some approach. Starting with the kind of idea in (1), the research could criticize it or fill in further details.

(3)   The project could be an AI experiment, where a theory as in (1) and (2) is applied to some domain. Such experiments are usually computer programs that implement a particular theory.

As Ritchie and Hanna acknowledge, most AI work falls into categories (2) and (3). Such is the case here as well: credit for (1) should go to [2-6].

This book describes an AI experiment: a multiyear effort investigating the application of a novel machine-learning technique in a particular domain. Experience with the design and implementation of a computer program embodying these machine-learning ideas helps us in developing a more complete theory. What steps can be taken to insure that this work is a contribution to forward progress in the greater scheme of AI rather than a forgotten side trip?

Ritchie and Hanna go on to note:

> It is one of the peculiarities of AI that, although replication of practical results is a cornerstone of traditional science, it is rare to see published accounts of repetitions of AI work. It is not clear how to interpret this phenomenon: it may be that few people have ever successfully re-implemented a large AI program, or it may be that those who do manage to repeat a published project do not regard this as publishable material. It may also be the case that an *unsuccessful* attempt at re-implementation would not be widely notified, since this might appear as an admission of incompetence. These circumstances impede the establishment of scientific standards within AI.

Here then lies the key: one way to insure that this experiment was not in vain is to prepare this document with a view towards the *rational reconstruction* of the program.

To this end, we now make the following promises (largely inspired by [7] and [8]):

(1)   To describe the theory behind the success of the system in a straightforward manner.

(2)   To describe this system in as code-free a fashion as possible, preferring to revert to pseudo-code descriptions of important algorithms rather than reprinting the implementation[1].

(3)   To give annotated examples of the system in operation which give helpful insights into the operation of particular parts of the code.

(4)   To avoid McDermott's third sin of AI research:

> Only in a cautious footnote does he say, "the program was never actually finished," or, "only a preliminary version of the program was actually written."

All of the examples in this document are the product of a single version of the system, and are reproduced without embellishment.[2]

---

[1] Our aim is to encourage rational reconstruction, not blind porting of computer code.

[2] McDermott calls this sin ** *Only a Preliminary Version of the Program was Actually Implemented*. The other sins discussed in [8] are *wishful mnemonics* and *unnatural language*. This is not meant to be an exhaustive list by any means.

Any judgement of the merits or success of this project must be based on the assumption that the technique here described (*explanation-based learning*) is a worthwhile addition to the machine-learning repertory. If one believes this to be the case, the validity of the work done and reported herein depends on meeting the following criteria:

(1) The description of the technique is thorough enough to give the reader a clear understanding of how it works.

(2) The experiment itself clearly establishes the relation between theory and practice (the implementation).

(3) The description of the program is thorough enough to permit the rational reconstruction and, therefore, the independent verification of this experiment.

If all of these criteria are met, then this research has accomplished its primary goal: to further elaborate and validate (by means of a prototype computer implementation in a nontrivial domain) a novel method of automatic knowledge acquisition.

Acknowledgements

This book describes research conducted over a four-year period while a graduate student in the Coordinated Science Laboratory of the University of Illinois at Urbana-Champaign.

The completion of the Ph.D. normally marks the end of a student career and the beginning of one's professional life. It therefore seems appropriate that this work be dedicated to my mother and father, the two people who have had the greatest influence on who and what I am today. Their love, support, and noble example have instilled in me the deepest feelings of love, gratitude, and respect. I am truly very fortunate in having two such extraordinary role models.

Many people contributed to this work in one way or another. I wish to thank my advisor, Professor Gerald DeJong, for his faith and trust in me. His insight and originality have time and time again provided that first dent in a problem's armor. Professors Narendra Ahuja, Edward Davidson, Kenneth Forbus, Franco Preparata, and Robert Stepp served on my preliminary and final examination committees, providing many worthwhile comments and suggestions for improvements. In addition, Professor David Waltz was influential in the early formative stages of this project. Whatever small amount of praise this work may merit, but for them it would deserve far less.

It is impossible to remain immersed in a particular problem for many years without a vital and stimulating research environment. This environment is, in large part, provided by my fellow graduate students in the Coordinated Science Laboratory, from both within and outside the Artificial Intelligence Research Group. Special thanks go to Scott Bennett, Gianfranco Bilardi, Steve Chien, Marcy Dorfman, Scot Hornick, Anthony Maddox, Bartlett Mel, Ray Mooney, Laura Neher, Jeff Yung-Choa Pan, Jordan Pollack, Ashwin Ram, Shankar Rajamoney, Jude Shavlik, David Spoor and Brad Whitehall for many profitable hours of discussion and interaction.

Professor Stephen Lu of the University of Illinois Department of Mechanical and Industrial Engineering contributed his much-appreciated robotics' expertise. Brad Gustafson, with the help of Paul Chen, was responsible for the real-world robot arm experiment.

Finally, I would be remiss in not acknowledging my friend, confidante, then fianceé and now wife, Lisa, for sharing the ups and downs of the final graduate-student year. She has made it so much more bearable and enjoyable.

Support for this research was provided by a Caterpillar Corporation Graduate Fellowship, the Air Force Office of Scientific Research under grant F49620-82-K-0009, and the National Science Foundation under grants NSF-IST-83-17889 and NSF-IST-85-11542.

A.M.S.

MACHINE LEARNING OF ROBOT ASSEMBLY PLANS

Chapter 1
Introduction

This book describes an experiment involving the application of a recently developed machine-learning technique, *explanation-based learning*, to the *robot retraining problem*. Explanation-based learning permits a system to acquire generalized problem-solving knowledge on the basis of a single observed problem-solving example. The description of the design and implementation of this experimental computer program serves as a vehicle for discussing issues related to this particular type of learning. This work clarifies and extends the corpus of knowledge so that explanation-based learning can be successfully applied to real-world problems.

The ability to generalize from examples in order to produce new, operational knowledge makes for a very powerful system. Since the very early days of artificial intelligence (AI) research, many AI researchers felt that the development of learning machines was their eventual goal:

> Our ultimate objective is to make programs that learn from their experience as effectively as humans do [9].

In fact, some AI researchers believe that the ability to learn lies at the very heart of intelligence:

> It should also be clear that an AI program that cannot build itself up gradually, without requiring all its knowledge stuffed in at the beginning, is not really intelligent [10].

Machine learning is precisely that subfield of AI which aims to understand this process.

1.1. Machine Learning

Why do we study machine learning? Any answer must rest on one of the most basic methodological assumptions of AI, the *knowledge representation hypothesis*:

> Any mechanically embodied intelligent process will be comprised of
> structural ingredients that (a) we as external observers naturally take
> to represent a propositional account of the knowledge that the overall
> process exhibits, and (b) independent of such external semantical attri-
> bution, play a formal but causal and essential role in engendering the
> behavior that manifests that knowledge [11].

Paraphrasing more simply:

> any intelligent system will require knowledge about its domain that is
> explicitly and recognizably encoded.

Apart from any controversy about what scheme should be used to
encode this domain knowledge,[3] there are real questions about how to
maintain consistency across the knowledge base. These systems have
tremendous potential for the adverse interaction of inconsistent
knowledge:

> Perhaps you know how knowledge is organized in your brain; I don't
> know how it's organized in mine. As a consequence, I think it would be
> exceedingly difficult for me to create new, debugged code that would be
> compatible with what is already stored there [12].

But consistency is only one of our concerns: if past experience with
microworlds is any indication, AI systems that are to operate in
restricted real-world environments will require staggering amounts of
domain knowledge. And as the restrictions are relaxed, the amount of
knowledge manipulated by such systems will grow still larger. This
raises some concern over the pragmatic aspect of building these large
quantities of domain-specific knowledge into a system:

> Perhaps the deepest legitimate reason for doing machine learning
> research is that, in the long run for big knowledge-based systems,
> learning will turn out to be more efficient than programming, however
> inefficient such learning is [12].

1.2. Robotics

The robot domain has long been a favorite for AI research. This is
due to the fact that it represents a real world domain, albeit with an
important restriction: industrial robots exist in a controlled
environment. Even with this restriction, the robot domain has been too
complex for most AI projects, forcing so many simplifying assumptions
that the experimental domain bears little resemblance to any real-world
application.

---

[3] This is still the open question of knowledge representation research.

1.2.1. Why Can't Robbie Learn?

Robots have the potential to revolutionize the manufacturing process. Unfortunately, the robot has yet to live up to expectations. While it is indeed a *general-purpose* device, it is far from the *flexible* automation tool it was first touted to be. This lack of flexibility is manifest in the difficulties encountered when preparing a robot to perform some novel task: we call this the *robot retraining problem*.

There are two general strategies in use today to address the robot retraining problem: *teach-by-guiding systems*, and *robot programming systems*. A good description of these systems with examples can be found in [13].

1.2.2. Teach-By-Guiding Systems

Teach-by-guiding systems are trained by leading the robot through the task it is to perform. Important points are marked during teaching and then replayed by the robot over and over again. These systems are also referred to as *tape-recorder mode* robot systems.

The greatest advantage of teach-by-guiding systems is that they are extremely easy to implement. In addition, in practical use it is only necessary to have a task expert do the teaching; it is fairly easy to train a task expert (such as a job foreman) how to use the teaching pendant on a commercially available robot. Their greatest disadvantage is the lack of any control constructs. For example, in the simpler systems, there is no way to repeat a given subsequence at different locations in the workspace. The absence of control structures that provide conditional branching precludes the use of iteration, and also makes any complex interaction with sensors difficult.

Extended guiding systems (also referred to as *hybrid systems* since they incorporate a mix of guiding and programming) attempt to resolve these difficulties by adding simple control structures and prepackaged sensor strategies to guiding systems. They fall short of full programming systems in that not all control strategies are supported, and only direct testing of sensor input values is permitted for conditional execution.

1.2.3. Robot Programming Systems

Robot programming systems provide a language for the construction of robot programs to guide the manipulator in the same way that computer programming languages are used to instruct a computer. These systems can be further divided into two general categories: *robot-level programming systems* and *task-level programming systems*.

Robot-level programming systems require that the user specify robot motion and sensor interaction. AML [14] is a good example of today's robot-level programming languages. The emphasis in AML is on developing a good, easily-customized user interface. The quality of the user interface is important, since the user must enter every detail of the robot's actions and sensory interaction.

Current research in robot programming is aimed at developing task-level programming systems where the user specifies higher-level constructs as they relate to the objects being manipulated in the workspace. The system then synthesizes the robot-level program that carries out the task given the current state of the world. This synthesis process, done by the *task planner*, is critically sensitive to the particular knowledge about the world that is built into the system. This knowledge must include not only information about the objects being manipulated, but also specific control strategies, including when and how to use sensors. In short, a task-level system relies on the user to specify an object-relative description of the steps in the assembly sequence, from which it then generates a robot-level program embodying the desired assembly sequence. Research in task-level systems is still fairly preliminary: no applications exist as yet outside the research laboratories.

1.2.4. Myopia on the Road to Intelligent Robots

Robot programming is not, however, a panacea. In conjunction with research on more advanced sensory devices (e.g., machine vision, tactile sensors), the robotics community has placed a great deal of emphasis on the construction of better programming languages and user interfaces. But robot-level programming languages must rely on the skill and foresight of human programmers for their apparent abilities to adapt to new situations. Even task-level systems rely on the human programmer to define the general strategy and ordering with which to attack the problem.

To define intelligence as

the ability to use information to modify system behavior in *preprogrammed* ways [14] (emphasis added)

is, at best, myopic. We do not ascribe the elusive trait *intelligence* to FORTRAN programs that invert large matrices, so why should we consider the end product of any robot programming tool (regardless of how sophisticated its user interface may be) to be intelligent?

In the final analysis, robot planning systems must inevitably (if only due to the sheer quantity of domain knowledge they require) face the knowledge acquisition bottleneck. At that point, the marriage between machine learning and robotics becomes a matter of absolute practical necessity.

1.3. About the Book

Described in this book is the computer program that resulted from an experimental application of explanation-based learning to a restricted robot manufacturing domain. The program is called *ARMS*, for *Acquiring Robotic Manufacturing Schemata* [15]. We feel that this experiment is an important contribution to artificial intelligence research for the following reasons:

(1) From the machine-learning perspective, it is an ambitious implementation of explanation-based learning. Unlike many other vehicles for machine-learning research, the ARMS system operates in a nontrivial domain conveying the flavor of a real robot assembly application. As such, ARMS has addressed the crucial open issues in explanation-based learning as no paper-and-pencil simulation can.

(2) From the robotics perspective, it represents an important first step towards a learning-apprentice system for manufacturing. It posits a theoretically more satisfactory solution to the robot retraining problem, and offers an eventual alternative to the limitations of robot programming.

1.3.1. Organization

We begin with an example from a robot assembly domain. This particular example serves as a framework for the discussion in the rest of the book. It is first introduced in Chapter 2, where discussion of the example is limited to a very intuitive level. The goal is to establish in the mind of the reader a concrete idea of what the system is capable of doing.

In Chapter 3 we present an overview of the theory of explanation-based learning. We begin by examining previous research in machine learning and then introduce the explanation-based learning paradigm.

Described in Chapter 4 is the domain of application for our explanation-based learning experiment, giving a full description of the robot domain manipulated by ARMS.

The discussion of Chapter 5 covers those knowledge representation issues relevant to ARMS, as well as a general description of the ARMS learning and problem-solving mechanisms.

The ARMS implementation is described in full detail in Chapter 6. This description is intended to permit the reconstruction of the ARMS system from scratch, and is, therefore, necessarily very technical in nature. As discussed in the preface, reconstruction is an important mechanism for independent verification of the validity of this research.

In Chapter 7 we revisit the example of Chapter 2. In it, we provide a more detailed description of the behavior of the ARMS system when presented with the same example.

In Chapter 8 we analyze the important issues addressed by this research. In it we outline the relation of ARMS to other systems, as well as directions for future research.

The appendices contain additional information related to this experiment. In Appendices A and B we provide helpful background information intended to help the reader unfamiliar with certain areas. In Appendices C and D we present two other examples from the same robot assembly domain as the example of Chapters 2 and 7. These examples are significantly different and serve to illustrate various issues and problems addressed by ARMS. The discussion of Appendix E presents empirical evidence of ARMS performance and how it supports the conclusions of the rest of the work. In Appendix F we provide a quick reference to the domain knowledge built into the ARMS system.

There are various approaches to reading this document. In every case, Chapter 2 should be read carefully. Those primarily interested in explanation-based learning issues should pay special attention to Chapters 3 and 5. The casual reader is encouraged to skip Chapter 6, as its technical nature limits its readibility. Those contemplating a reconstruction effort should, of course, study Chapter 6. Chapters 7 and 8 should be perused by all readers.

1.3.2. On the Use of the $ Symbol

The alert reader will no doubt notice the use of the special symbol "$" as the first character of certain words throughout the book. This symbol is used to indicate that the item is a data structure. Often the characters following the "$" contain sufficient information for the reader to infer what the data structure represents. For more information about the proper use of this special symbol, see Section 6.1.

Chapter 2
Scenario

In this chapter we examine a transcript of the ARMS system in operation. The emphasis here is in providing an intuitive feel for the operation of the system; later, we will revisit the same example and provide more detail.

The system, acting as an *apprentice*, learns how to assemble simple mechanisms by observing an external problem-solving agent. In this example, we will see a human expert guiding the robot arm step by step through a solution to an assembly problem which the system was not able to solve. As the system observes the expert's solution, it constructs an internal *explanation* of why the expert's solution successfully solves the problem. A generalized version of the explanation is added to the system's knowledge base, where it is later used by the system to automatically generate solutions (sequences of robot arm commands) for similar tasks.

2.1. Preliminaries

Before we begin the transcript, there is some essential background information we must supply about the robot arm and the assembly being constructed. The domain consists of a simple disembodied two-fingered robot gripper moving about a set of pieces sitting on a workspace surface. The pieces are assembled into a mechanism that demonstrates a well-defined mechanical behavior.

2.1.1. The Widget

Consider the simple *widget*[4] mechanism illustrated in Figure 2.1.[5]

_____

[4] We use the term *widget* throughout this book to describe the type of

It consists of three pieces: a peg, a washer, and a block. The three pieces in this particular set will be represented by the data structures $Peg1, $Washer1, and $BoredBlock1, respectively.

The widget is assembled by aligning $Washer1 over the hole in $BoredBlock1 and then inserting the shaft of $Peg1 through both of the other pieces. Once assembled, $Washer1 spins freely about the shaft of $Peg1, but is restricted in any sliding motion along this shaft by collisions with the underside of the head of $Peg1 on one side and the upper surface of $BoredBlock1 on the other.

This kind of mechanical behavior can be described as a *revolute joint* between $Washer1 and $BoredBlock1. A revolute joint has a one and only one *degree of freedom* (a *revolute* degree of freedom) between its two pieces.

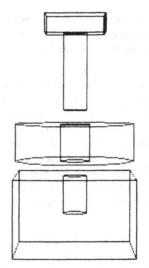

Exploded View of Widget Assembly

Figure 2.1

---

peg/washer/block assembly shown in Figure 2.1.

[5] Figure 2.1, like all of the other figures in this document, is reproduced directly from system output. It consists of a perspective projection of the current state of the workspace. Each piece is represented as a wireframe without the benefit of a hidden line removal algorithm.

2.1.2. Moving the Robot Arm

The system manipulates an abstract, idealized, model of a robot arm. We are not concerned with the geometry of the arm itself, but only with the position and orientation of the end-effector that in this case is a two-fingered gripper. Thus the state of the arm can be completely specified by giving the Cartesian location of the gripper *hot-spot* (the point directly between the tips of the two fingers) along with the orientation of the hand. In addition, one must specify whether the fingers are opened or closed.

This idealized arm is capable of executing five robot arm commands:

(1) *Open:* Open the gripper fingers.

(2) *Close:* Close the gripper fingers.

(3) *Translate (unitVector, delta):* Move the gripper in a straight line.

(4) *Rotate (unitVector, theta):* Rotate the gripper about an axis.

(5) *MoveTo (newPosition):* Move the gripper to a new position along some free path.

All input to the robot arm is given as a sequence of instances of these commands with all their parameters (e.g., unitVector, theta, etc.) bound. These instances are also represented with data structures such as $Translate and $Rotate.

2.2. Specifying the Problem

Now we are ready to give the system a problem to solve. An ARMS problem specification consists of two parts: an *initial state description* and a *functional goal specification*.

2.2.1. Describing the Initial State

Figure 2.2 shows an initial placement of the widget pieces on the workspace surface. $BoredBlock1 is on the right, with its socket also facing towards the right. $Washer1 is in the foreground, with $Peg1 stacked on top of it. In addition, there is a fourth piece (hereafter $Block1) in the left rear part of the workspace which, as we shall soon see, does not belong to the finished widget. The disembodied robot arm gripper is shown in its home position as a two-fingered palm with the two (closed) fingers pointed downwards.

This particular placement is one of an infinite number of legal initial piece placements possible for these four pieces. The physical specifications of the pieces, along with their positions relative to the workspace frame of reference, constitute the *initial state* specification for

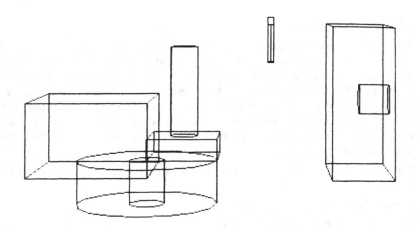

Initial State for Widget Assembly Problem

The disembodied robot arm gripper is located in the center of the picture with its fingers closed and pointing downwards. $BoredBlock1 is off to the right, with its socket also pointing to the right. $Block1 is in the left rear of the picture. $Peg1 is stacked on top of $Washer1 in the foreground, just left of center.

Figure 2.2

the system.

2.2.2. Specifying the Goal State

At this point we specify a *goal state* for the system to achieve. The goal state is specified by a shorthand description of the data structure representing the desired *function* of the completed widget assembly:

$RevoluteJoint($Washer1, $BoredBlock1)

rather than by a physical description (e.g., the mating conditions of the assembled pieces). This functional goal specification is a much more natural way to specify a mechanism, since the designer need not be overly concerned with details of the mechanism's physical appearance.

The shorthand notation used for specifying a mechanism's function describes the behavior of one piece ($Washer1 in this case) with respect to another ($BoredBlock1). The type of behavior is implicit in the predicate $RevoluteJoint; in this case it describes a simple rotation of $Washer1 with respect to $BoredBlock1 about an axis. This rotation is the only motion of $Washer1 with respect to $BoredBlock1 permitted by the mechanism.

2.3. Attempting to Solve the Problem

Given this complete problem specification, the system attempts to generate a solution to the problem. A solution consists of a sequence of robot arm commands which, when executed beginning from the initial state, produce a mechanical assembly with the desired functional property. In this case, the system fails to solve the problem for two reasons:

(1) the system does not know of any mechanical assemblies that have the desired functional property, and

(2) the system has no idea what sequence of operations to use to put the pieces together.

2.4. Observing the Expert's Plan

Once the system has failed to generate a solution, control is transferred to the expert so that the system may be shown a valid solution. On the factory floor, the solution sequence would presumably be given by a factory foreman through some sort of teach-pendant device.

We now follow along as the expert leads the system through an assembly episode that results in the successful assembly of the widget from the starting position of Figure 2.2. There are a total of 30 robot arm commands in this sequence. Figures 2.3 through 2.15 show some of the intermediate workspace configurations during execution of the observed command sequence.

There are three especially interesting quirks in the expert's plan:

(1) While removing $Peg1 from of the top of $Washer1 (Figures 2.6 through 2.8), the expert chooses to move the arm using four $Translate commands (along Z, X, Y, and negative Z axes, respectively) where a single $MoveTo would do as well. Due to the implementations of these primitives on most industrial arms, the computational expense of a $MoveTo is always much less than a $Translate.

(2) $Peg1 is transferred to the top of $Block1 (Figure 2.8) rather than simply placing it directly on the workspace surface. This would condemn a normal teach-by-guiding robot arm to reliance on the presence of this redundant piece.

(3) Before grasping $Washer1, the expert directs the arm to execute a $Rotate command (Figure 2.10), twisting the gripper 90 degrees around the vertical axis. This twist is redundant, since by the symmetry of $Washer1 it makes no difference what two points on its exterior surface are grasped by the robot gripper so long as they are diametrically opposed.

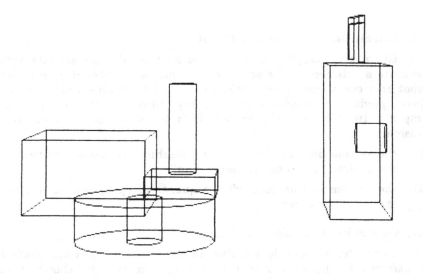

$MoveTo, $Open

The gripper is positioned over $BoredBlock1 with a $MoveTo command. The gripper fingers are then opened to their maximum aperture with an $Open command.

Figure 2.3

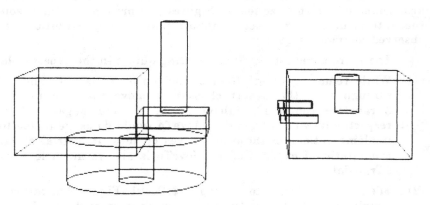

$Translate, $Close, $MoveTo

The gripper is lowered over $BoredBlock1 using a $Translate command. The subsequent $Close command closes the gripper fingers until they make contact with two opposing faces of $BoredBlock1. A $MoveTo command is then used to reposition $BoredBlock1.

Figure 2.4

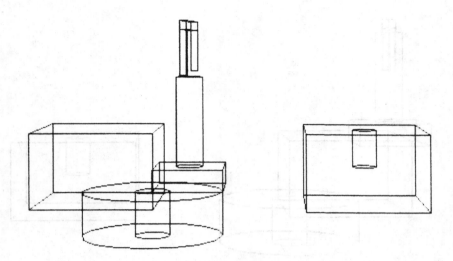

$Open, $Translate, $MoveTo

The $Open command is used to drop $BoredBlock1 at its new position. The gripper is backed away from $BoredBlock1 with a $Translate command, and then approaches $Peg1 from above with a $MoveTo.

Figure 2.5

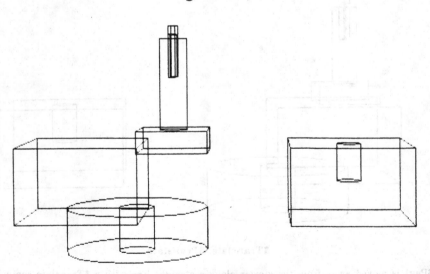

$Translate, $Close, $Translate

The gripper is lowered over the shaft of $Peg1. The fingers are closed, grasping $Peg1 by diametrically opposing spots on the cylindrical shaft. $Peg1 is then raised straight up from $Washer1 with a $Translate.

Figure 2.6

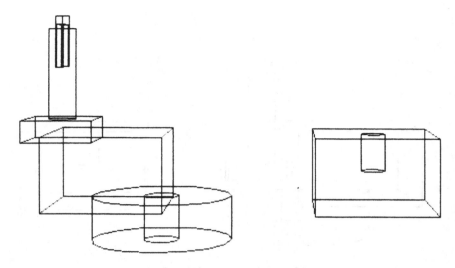

$Pegl is moved to the left along a straight line with a $Translate command.

Figure 2.7

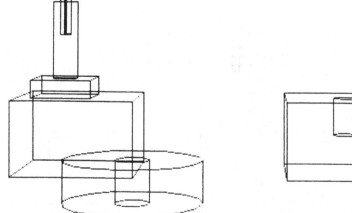

$Translate, $Translate

$Pegl is moved away from the viewer along a straight line with a $Translate command, and then lowered straight down onto $Block1 with another $Translate command.

Figure 2.8

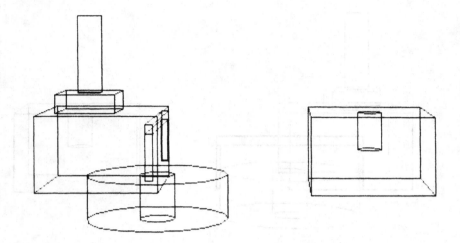

$Open, $Translate, $MoveTo

$Peg1 is dropped on top of $Block1 with an $Open command. The gripper then backs up away from $Peg1 with a $Translate and approaches $Washer1 from above with a $MoveTo.

Figure 2.9

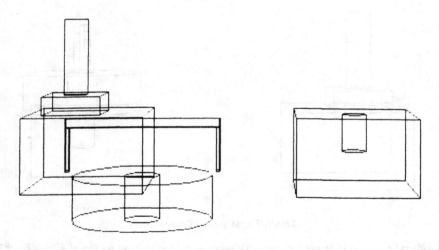

$Rotate

The gripper is rotated by ninety degrees about a vertical axis.

Figure 2.10

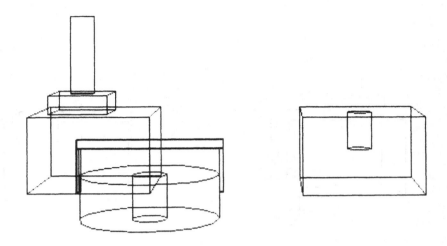

$Translate, $Close

The gripper is lowered, using a $Translate, so as to surround $Washer1. The fingers are closed with a $Close command, grasping $Washer1 by diametrically opposing spots on $Washer1's exterior cylindrical surface.

Figure 2.11

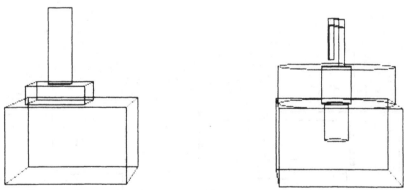

$MoveTo, $Open, $Translate

A $MoveTo command is used to move $Washer to a new position on top of $BoredBlock1. The $Open command drops $Washer1, and a $Translate is used to back up away from $Washer1.

Figure 2.12

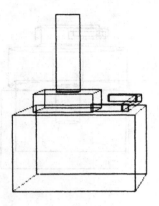 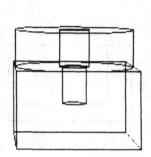

$MoveTo

The $MoveTo command repositions the gripper facing the side of $Peg1's head.

Figure 2.13

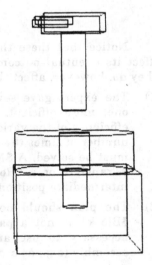

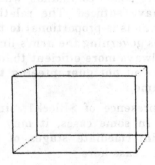

$Translate, $Close, $MoveTo

A $Translate moves the gripper to the left along a straight line until it surrounds the head of $Peg1. The $Close command grasps $Peg1, and a $MoveTo is used to reposition $Peg1 over $Washer1.

Figure 2.14

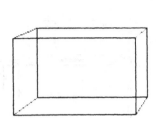 

$Translate

The $Translate command moves $Peg1 down along a vertical axis until it is inserted
through $Washer1 into $BoredBlock1.

Figure 2.15

Notice that these three shortcomings in the expert's plan do not
affect its eventual outcome: the widget is still assembled successfully.
They do, however, affect the plan's *efficiency*:

(1)   The expert gave several inefficient $Translate commands where
      one, more efficient, $MoveTo would have sufficed. The relative
      efficiency of the various robot arm commands is proportional to the
      number of times the kinematic equations governing the arm's links
      must be solved. A $MoveTo is almost always more efficient than a
      $Translate or a $Rotate, at the expense of not guaranteeing the
      intermediate positions the arm will assume.

(2)   The plan should not depend on the presence of $Block1, since
      $Block1 is not a part of the widget. In some cases, it may be
      necessary to use an extra piece in intermediate stages of an
      assembly (e.g., as a prop), but this not the case here.

(3)   The expert's use of the $Rotate command is unnecessary, as it does
      not contribute to achieving the requisite $RevoluteJoint.

2.5. Generalizing the Solution

The system adds a generalized version of the expert's solution to
its knowledge base. The generalization process relies on the initial state
description, the functional goal description, the observed sequence of
robot arm commands, and the final state determined by executing the

robot arm commands supplied by the expert. It also relies on the system's domain-specific knowledge to tie all of these elements together.

2.6. Solving the Same Problem After Learning

We again pose the original functional goal specification with the same initial state as Figure 2.2. This time, the system is able to generate a robot arm command sequence that successfully assembles the widget. The system's solution consists of 24 robot arm commands: 6 less than the observed sequence provided by the expert. The new solution does not rely on the presence of $Block1, nor does it insert redundant commands like the $Rotate of Figure 2.10. In addition, the sequence formulated by the system uses the most efficient robot arm commands possible, preferring to clear $Peg1 using a single $MoveTo rather than a set of four $Translates. Note, however, that the system recognizes the importance of the $Translate of Figure 2.15 to the success of the plan, and does not replace it with a more efficient but, in this case ineffective, $MoveTo.[6]

Now consider the initial piece placement of Figure 2.16. Note that $Block1 does not appear in this initial configuration. In addition, note that the starting positions for $Peg1, $Washer1 and $BoredBlock1 have been changed.

The system is again given:

$RevoluteJoint($Washer1, $BoredBlock1)

as a functional goal specification. By applying the generalized plan just acquired, the system is able to generate an assembly sequence of just 12 robot arm commands to assemble the widget from this initial state (see Figures 2.16 through 2.21).

---

[6] We are assuming that $MoveTo requires fewer kinematic solutions and, therefore, is always more efficient than a $Translate or $Rotate. Recall that, unlike $Translate or $Rotate, $MoveTo does not guarantee a *particular* arm trajectory but simply a final gripper position and orientation. When inserting $Peg1 into $Washer1 and $BoredBlock1, the trajectory followed by the gripper is crucial.

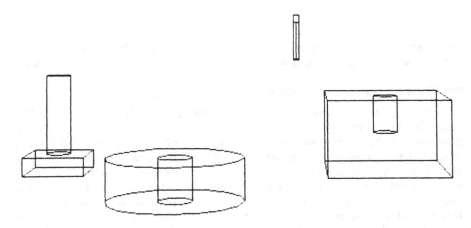

First Alternate Initial State for Widget Assembly Problem

The robot gripper is located in the center of the picture with fingers closed. $BoredBlock1 is to the right, $Peg1 is to the left, and $Washer1 is in the foreground just left of center.

Figure 2.16

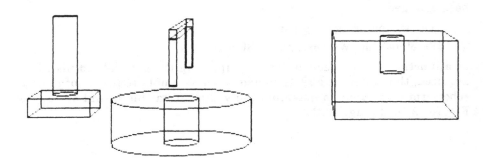

$MoveTo, $Open

The gripper is moved to a position above $Washer1 with a $MoveTo. The $Open command opens the gripper fingers to their maximum aperture.

Figure 2.17

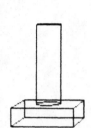
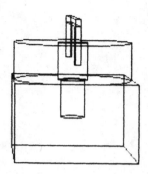

$Translate, $Close $MoveTo

The gripper is moved downward in a straight line with a $Translate in order to surround $Washer1. The $Close command grasps $Washer1 by diametrically opposed points on its exterior cylindrical surface. The $MoveTo moves $Washer1 to its new position atop $BoredBlock1.

Figure 2.18

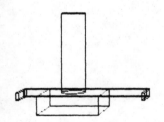
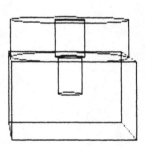

$Open, $Translate, $MoveTo

The $Open command drops $Washer1 on $BoredBlock1. The $Translate backs the gripper away from $Washer1, and the $MoveTo repositions the gripper facing the head of $Peg1.

Figure 2.19

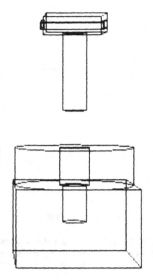

$Translate, $Close, $MoveTo

The gripper surrounds the head of $Peg1 with a $Translate. The $Close command grasps $Peg1, while $MoveTo positions $Peg1 above $Washer1.

Figure 2.20

$Translate

The $Translate command moves $Peg1 along a vertical axis until it is inserted through $Washer1 into $BoredBlock1.

Figure 2.21

In Figure 2.22, we note the addition of a new piece, $Block2, to $Peg1, $Washer1 and $BoredBlock1. $Block2 and $Peg1 are both sitting on top of $Washer1. Notice also that, like the situation in Figure 2.16, the starting positions of $Peg1, $Washer1, and $BoredBlock1 have been changed from the situation of Figure 2.2.

Again we give the system:

$RevoluteJoint($Washer1, $BoredBlock1)

as a functional goal specification. The system generates a command sequence of 30 steps to assemble the widget from this, initially more complex, starting state (see Figures 2.22 through 2.31).

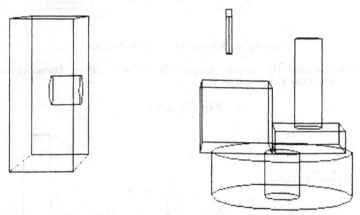

Second Alternate Initial State for Widget Assembly Problem

The robot gripper is located in the center of the picture with fingers closed. $BoredBlock1 is to the left. $Washer1 is to the right, with $Block2 and $Peg1 stacked on top of it.

Figure 2.22

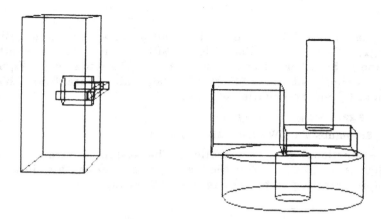

$MoveTo, $Open, $Translate, $Close

The $MoveTo positions the gripper facing $BoredBlock1. The $Translate surrounds $BoredBlock1, while the $Close grasps it.

Figure 2.23

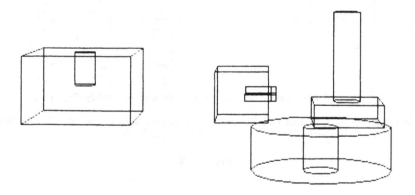

$MoveTo, $Open, $Translate, $MoveTo, $Translate, $Close, $MoveTo

The $MoveTo and $Open deposit $BoredBlock1 on its back with its socket pointing up. The $Translate backs away from $BoredBlock1, while the following $MoveTo, $Translate and $Close achieve a grasping of $Block2. The last $MoveTo places $Block2 in a free spot at the back of the workspace.

Figure 2.24

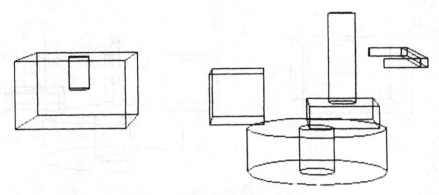

$Open, $Translate, $MoveTo

The **$Open** command drops $Block2 in the background, while the subsequent $MoveTo leaves the gripper facing the shaft of $Peg1.

Figure 2.25

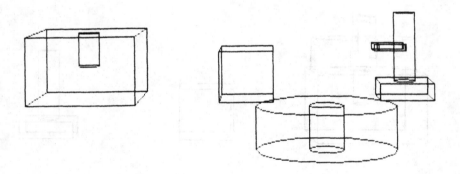

$Translate, $Close, $MoveTo

The **$Translate** and **$Close** achieve grasp $Peg1 by diametrically opposed points on its shaft. The **$MoveTo** positions $Peg1 at a free spot at the back of the workspace.

Figure 2.26

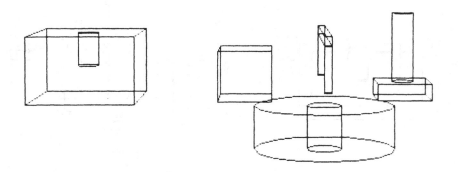

$Open, $Translate, $MoveTo

The $Open and $Translate drop $Peg1 and back the gripper away from it. The $MoveTo leaves the gripper facing $Washer1 from above.

Figure 2.27

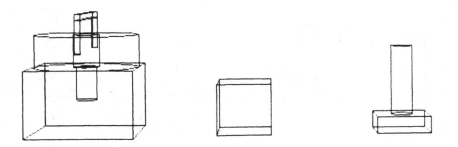

$Translate, $Close, $MoveTo

The gripper approaches $Washer1 with a $Translate, and then the $Close grasps it. The $MoveTo places $Washer1 on top of $BoredBlock1 with their holes aligned.

Figure 2.28

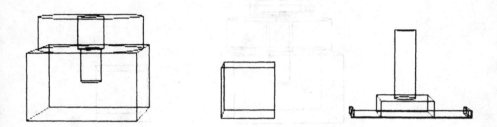

$Open, $Translate, $MoveTo

The $Open and $Translate drop $Washer1 and back away from it. The $MoveTo approaches the head of $Peg1 from the front.

Figure 2.29

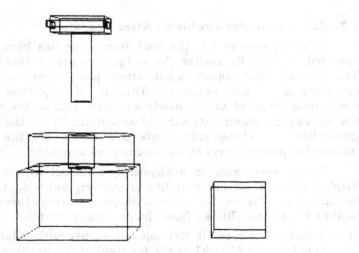

$Translate, $Close, $MoveTo

$Translate and $Close grasp $Peg1, while the $MoveTo positions it aligned above $Washer1.

Figure 2.30

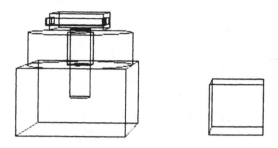

$Translate

The final $Translate inserts $Peg1 through $Washer1 into $BoredBlock1.

Figure 2.31

2.7. Solving Similar Problems After Learning

In every case so far, the goal description has been only partially specified: to actually realize the widget requires a third piece, $Peg1. The system must decide what other piece(s) are involved in the construction of the assembly. This is accomplished by matching constraints attached to the newly acquired plan to the extra pieces in the workspace, constraints derived automatically by the system during generalization. These constraints are based on the function the unspecified piece(s) plays in the mechanical assembly.

In the next example, a physically different widget is constructed displaying the same functionality as our original widget. Consider the initial state of Figure 2.32. The workspace contains three new pieces as well as $Peg1 and $Block1 from the previous example.

(1) $Washer2 is a small, flat, square washer with a large round hole. It is lying on $Block1 at the far right of the workspace.

(2) $Peg3 consists of a cylindrical shaft with a slightly larger cylindrical head. It is also lying, shaft pointing upwards, on top of $Block1, just to the left of $Washer2. Note that the shaft of $Peg3 is fatter and shorter than the shaft of $Peg1.

(3) $BoredCylinder1 is much like $BoredBlock1, except that the hole is bored into a large cylinder instead of a large block.

The system is given

$RevoluteJoint($Washer2, $BoredCylinder1)

as the functional goal specification. By applying the generalized plan just acquired, the system is able to plan the assembly sequence for this never-before-seen new widget. Also note that the goal specification is once again incomplete, as it is missing any reference to any peg, much less $Peg3. The selection of $Peg3, over the other unused pieces in the workspace ($Block1 or the training example's $Peg1), is based on constraints derived from the function of the original widget. These functional constraints are translated into necessary physical characteristics that constrain the peg choice. The 18-sequence plan generated by the system is illustrated in Figures 2.32 through 2.38.

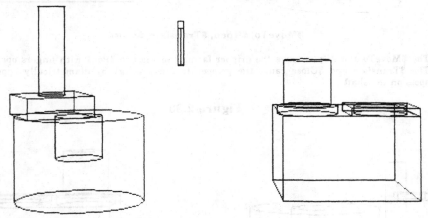

Third Alternate Initial State for Widget Assembly Problem

The robot gripper is located in the center of the picture with fingers closed. $Bored-Cylinder1 is to the left, with $Peg1 stacked on top of it. $Peg3 and $Washer2 are stacked (from left to right) on top of $Block1 on the right side of the workspace.

Figure 2.32

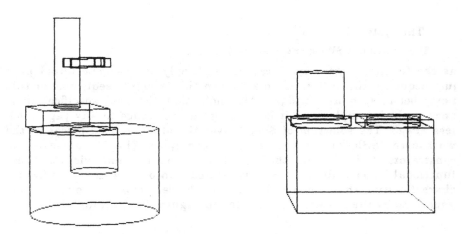

$MoveTo, $Open, $Translate, $Close

The $MoveTo and $Open leave the gripper facing the shaft of $Peg1 with fingers opened. The $Translate and $Close cause the gripper to grasp $Peg1 by diametrically opposed spots on the shaft.

Figure 2.33

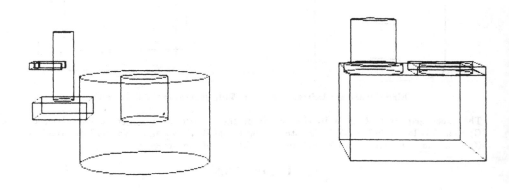

$MoveTo

The $MoveTo positions $Peg1 at the left rear of the workspace.

Figure 2.34

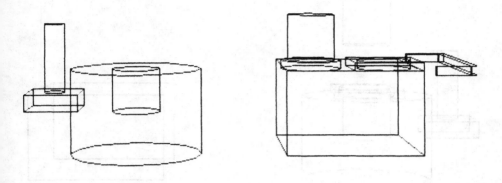

$Open, $Translate, $MoveTo

The $Open and $Translate drop $Peg1, while the subsequent $MoveTo positions the gripper facing $Washer2.

Figure 2.35

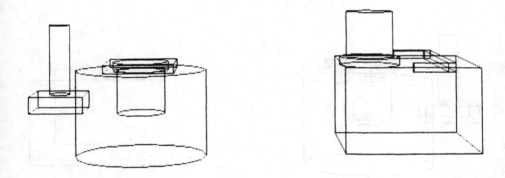

$Translate, $Close, $MoveTo, $Open, $Translate, $MoveTo

$Translate and $Close accomplish the grasping of $Washer2. The $MoveTo positions $Washer2 on top of $BoredCylinder1. $Open and $Translate drop $Washer2 and back away from it, while the last $MoveTo leaves the gripper facing the head of $Peg3.

Figure 2.36

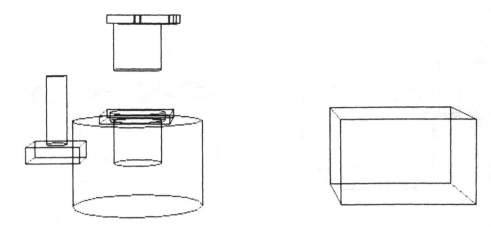

$Translate, $Close, $MoveTo

The $Translate and $Close grasp $Peg3 by diametrically opposing points on its cylindrical head. The $MoveTo positions $Peg3 above $Washer2.

Figure 2.37

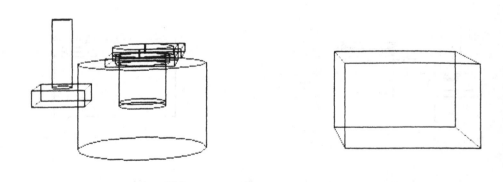

$Translate

The final $Translate accomplishes the insertion of $Peg3 through $Washer2 into $Bored-Cylinder1.

Figure 2.38

The important points to note are

(1) The generalized plan is insensitive to initial piece placements.

(2) The system can generate plans for complex initial piece placements, such as in Figure 2.22.

(3) The plans generated by the system ignore extra pieces in the workspace, even if the training example contains such useless dependencies (see initial state of Figure 2.16).

(4) The system generates plans that contain only necessary steps, even if the training example contains useless extra steps.

(5) The system is cognizant of the operational efficiency of the plan: it attempts to generate an efficient assembly sequence, often improving on the observed plan.

(6) The system can generate assembly plans for assemblies which are *functionally* similar, yet *physically* different, as demonstrated by the widget of Figure 2.32.

(7) The system generates constraints that can be used to guide the completion of missing information in the goal specification. These constraints on physical characteristics of the pieces involved in the assembly are derived from functional considerations.

Chapter 3
Explanation-Based Learning

The mechanism by which the ARMS system increases its planning ability belongs to that category of machine learning known as *explanation-based learning* (hereafter EBL) [2-6]. Explanation-based learning is a fairly recent addition to the machine-learning toolbox; relatively few systems have been implemented, and most are small prototypes.

In this chapter we examine previous research in machine learning, introduce the EBL paradigm, and prepare a framework for discussion of the ARMS system.

3.1. Similarity-Based Learning

Initially, machine-learning research focused primarily on *similarity-based learning* (SBL) systems, i.e., systems which rely on inductive inference for generalization [16]. Systems using these techniques are particularly well suited to *classification tasks*, where the goal is to determine whether or not an example belongs to a given solution class. Classification tasks can be contrasted with *problem-solving tasks*, or those tasks characterized by the application of a series of operators to cause changes in the state of the system's domain.

3.1.1. Applying SBL to Classification Tasks

A good example of a classification task is medical diagnosis [17]. The system generates a *rule* to be used for classifying future examples on the basis of a *training set* of correctly classified examples. Each example is described using a *feature set* of attribute/value pairs. Given a large and varied enough training set (e.g., case records and correct diagnoses), performance of such correlational learning systems in classifying new cases can actually exceed that of rules derived manually in collaboration with a human expert [18]. It was precisely this kind of system that provided the impetus for machine-learning research in its early years.

There are, however, a number of assumptions implicit in SBL:

(1)   The training set must be a representative sample of the underlying process that will generate future examples presented for classification. By preselecting members of the training set from a larger set based on some difference metric and by increasing the size of the training set itself the accuracy of the rule increases.

(2)   The training set must be correct. Most SBL systems do not tolerate noise or inconsistent training sets.

(3)   The feature set must be large enough to discriminate between positive and negative instances of the concept.

(4)   Correlational evidence is sufficient for the inductive step, and explicit causal relations are not generally considered. In some cases the quality of the generated rule may rely on the presence of negative training instances along with positive training instances.

As noted above, the performance and accuracy of the induced rule increases with the sizes of the training set and the feature set. Unfortunately, these increases have an adverse effect on the time necessary to induce a rule that adequately classifies the examples. For the more naive algorithms, this measure increases as the product of the feature set size and a combinatorial function of the training set size [19].

By adding heuristics to the induction algorithm (at the expense of the global optimality of solutions), the complexity can be reduced, although this makes any complexity analysis difficult. Empirical evidence, at least, lends credence to the claim that the addition of heuristics allows the complexity to approach linear growth with the product of the feature set and training set sizes [20].

It is possible to reduce an SBL system's dependence on having a training set that has been classified completely correctly. Most current SBL systems encompass some sort of probabilistic mechanism to reduce this sensitivity to noise in the training set [21].

One of the problems with classical SBL techniques is the *inductive leap* problem described above. Consider, for example, attempting to induce a rule that describes a classification of "terrorist" on the basis of accounts of terrorist acts. Further assume that, in every case, the terrorist carried a gun and wore blue jeans. Since the correlational evidence for these two features is identical, a naive system would have no reason to prefer one discriminating feature over the other.

There are two ways out: one is to include a *constraining instance* in the training set (e.g., terrorist with gun but without blue jeans), or else rely on what the system knows about the domain (terrorism) that makes guns relevant and blue jeans less so. This reliance on domain knowledge is crucial for guiding the inductive step. Naturally, in some domains no adequate domain theory exists to explain why things work the way they do: in these cases reliance on correlational evidence is the only current solution.[7] This example illustrates the utility of domain knowledge in creating proper classifications: the importance of domain knowledge increases when considering nonstatic tasks such as those presented in problem-solving domains.

3.1.2. Applying SBL to Problem-Solving Tasks

Up to now we have considered SBL in the context of classification tasks: how can SBL techniques be applied to problem-solving tasks?

The common approach to problem-solving tasks is to apply a *weak method*: a domain-independent method that searches for a path from a given initial state to a given goal state. Consider the problem space as a tree rooted at the initial state, where each node is a world state and each link is a possible operator applied to that world state. A weak method is a way to traverse the tree from the root to the goal leaf in the tree. Most search strategies (e.g., breadth-first, depth-first) are weak methods.

The *combinatorial explosion* refers to the growth in the size of the search tree that is linear with the number of possible operator combinations, and therefore exponential with the number of operators in the system. This characteristic precludes the use of weak methods for any but the smallest of search spaces.

How can SBL be used to improve the performance of a weak method problem solver? By modifying a weak method to use a domain-dependent evaluation strategy, the path taken down the tree can be directed along the paths most likely (as determined by our evaluation function) to lead to the goal. This reduces the need for backtracking and therefore increases the efficiency of the search. Best-first search is an example of such a heuristic method that retains full backtracking capability. Beam search provides only limited backtracking capabilities, and in the trivial case (hill climbing) removes backtracking capability altogether. Building good domain heuristics is not an easy task; however, by using SBL to induce the heuristics for operator applications,

---

[7] There has been some work in extending and/or correcting naive domain theories [22].

it is possible to improve the performance of the weak method.

Indeed, this is exactly the approach taken by [23, 24] in the domain of symbolic integration. The system examines the tree produced by a weak-method problem solver as it searches for a solution and induces new application heuristics for the operators. If the heuristics learned are perfect, e.g., if they lead directly to the goal without ever examining a bad branch, the performance of the search is linear in the number of operators that must be applied.

Approaching linear behavior requires the most effective heuristics possible. The success of the system relies on examining a large number of training instances. Negative instances correspond to the unsuccessfully expanded nodes in the search tree. If the system is examining a search tree produced by a weak-method problem solver (as in [23, 24]) this does not present a great problem: the weak-method problem solver will undoubtedly examine some bad branches that can then be used as negative instances. These serve the same purpose as the constraining instances described before: they keep the system from overgeneralizing or from making the wrong inductive leap.

All is not well, however. One of the problems with the SBL approach to learning in problem-solving domains is that learning from the search tree provided by a weak-method problem solver is needlessly limiting. A much more natural source for learning input is the behavior of an external, more expert, problem-solving agent. Unfortunately, this means that the necessary constraining instances, that were previously readily available from the weak-method problem solver, must now be provided by the external agent. This has the following shortcomings:

(1) Provision of constraining instances is introspective: the external agent often cannot give such introspective analysis correctly.

(2) Provision of constraining instances is invasive: the external agent cannot go about his problem-solving tasks without being bothered by the system. This obtrusiveness may be worse than bothersome: it may actually degrade the performance of the problem-solving agent.

There are other problems with this approach as well. Acquiring application heuristics is not the only learning technique possible for problem-solving tasks. It is simply the most straightforward when dealing with SBL methods. In fact, this approach simply reduces the problem-solving task to a classification task where the object is to classify a particular operator by its applicability.

Another well-known technique, first introduced by the STRIPS system [25], involves the acquisition of *problem-solving macro operators*, or *MACROPs*, that describe a sequence of operators as a single new operator. This is equivalent to packaging a path through the search tree as a single operator. This is an efficacious approach that removes some of the complexity of the planner's search by giving it more powerful operators to accomplish a goal in a single step. An SBL technique for learning MACROPs has yet to be developed.

3.2. Learning-Apprentice Systems

At this point we summarize the desirable criteria for a system that can improve its problem-solving behavior via observation:

(1) The system should not be limited by computational limits on a weak-method problem solver. It should be able to learn by analyzing the performance of a more powerful, external problem solver.

(2) The system should be capable of acquiring useful knowledge in one trial.

(3) The system should not require constraining instances.

(4) The system should rely on a domain theory, and not solely on correlational evidence, to guide the inductive step.

(5) The system should be able to acquire not only application conditions for existing operators, but new macro operators as well.

We term systems which meet these criteria *learning-apprentice systems*. Mitchell *et al* posit the following definition for a learning-apprentice system [26]:

> An *interactive* knowledge-based consultant that directly assimilates new problem-solving knowledge by observing and analyzing the problem-solving steps contributed by its users through their normal use of the system.

While this is an adequate definition, it does not make any statement about the invasiveness of the system. We prefer to use the following definition:

> A learning apprentice is a system, usually embedded in the software tools used by a human expert, that gradually increases its own problem-solving abilities by unobtrusively monitoring and analyzing the performance of the expert.

3.3. Explanation-Based Learning

Explanation-based systems are being applied to both classification tasks [23, 27] and problem-solving tasks [28-32]. When applied to the latter, they fulfill the requirements outlined above for a learning apprentice. Explanation-based learning systems are capable of acquiring knowledge from a single example. Using a domain theory, a successful problem solution is analyzed in order to explain how the goal is accomplished. This analysis, or *explanation*, is then generalized and used in future problem-solving activity.

The advantages of explanation-based learning are obvious:

(1)   EBL requires only a single example.

(2)   EBL can learn from a less than optimal successful solution: no expert teacher is required, just an adequate problem solution.

(3)   EBL need not be invasive.

(4)   EBL generalizations are correct if the domain theory is complete and correct.

(5)   EBL does not suffer from the inductive leap problem of SBL, which results from overreliance on correlational evidence.

Thus given a successful problem-solving episode and a complete and correct domain theory, EBL produces a correct generalization which covers the problem-solving behavior embodied in the example. Naturally, should the domain theory not be complete or correct, the quality of the generalizations produced by the system will suffer.

Consider, for example, a domain theory based on the Bohr model of the atom.[8] The Bohr atom is an adequate model that accounts for many atomic properties, such as the binding together of various atoms. It is not a correct model, but rather a naive model: as such, it would produce adequate explanations (and hence generalizations) for those phenomena which do not rely on the quantum mechanical properties of the atom. Much work in AI is devoted to the development of such naive process models [34, 35].

Some domains are less amenable to EBL than others. The medical diagnosis system described briefly above is a good example of a system in just such a domain. Our domain theory for, say, diseases of the blood is very limited: a real understanding of the causality involved in the various diseases and their chemical treatment is currently beyond medical science. In such domains, it is more reasonable to revert to SBL techniques that do not require a causal domain theory.

3.4. A Prototypical EBL System

The *Prototypical Explanation-Based Learning System* (hereafter referred to as PEBLS) as shown in Figure 3.1 consists of two elements

---

[8] This example borrowed from [33].

that do not operate concurrently: a *performance element* and a *learning element*. Both access *domain knowledge* contained in the *schema library*.

A *schema* [36-39] is a chunked knowledge structure that represents the system's generalized knowledge about a particular concept or topic. Schemata are used to represent, among other things, the *operators* that may be applied to the system's domain.[9] Each operator effects changes in the current state of the world. The current world state is described by a collection of *state schemata* that are partial descriptions of the world state, each representing a particular relation that holds in the current context. The relations expressed are often between *descriptors*, that represent a static concept (such as a physical object).

Recall that an explanation-based learning system *observes* examples of problem-solving behavior. This problem-solving behavior may be that of the system's own performance element or that of an outside expert. If the system observes its own behavior (usually from a

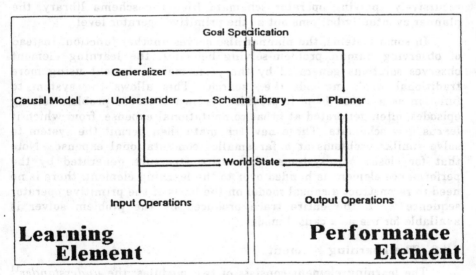

Prototypical Explanation-Based Learning System (PEBLS)

Figure 3.1

---

[9] Also sometimes termed *actions* or *events* in the planning literature.

weak-method problem solver), it can be termed a *closed-loop* learning system. If, on the other hand, the system learns by observing another problem-solving agent's performance we call it an *open-loop* learning system.

3.4.1. The Performance Element

The performance element applies known schemata towards the solution of a given problem. The problem is specified as a goal state to achieve, as well as the initial state from which to achieve it. The performance element provides a benchmark for learning.[10]

The performance element consists of a single module, the *planner*. Using known schemata, the planner supplies a sequence of operators to achieve the specified goal starting from the initial world state. The planner is a heuristic problem solver, often of the kind referred to as a *schema planner*.

Operator schemata in the schema library are indexed by the goal(s) they achieve. By dividing the task up into subgoals, and recursively applying operator schemata from the schema library, the planner eventually bottoms out at the primitive operator level.

In some systems, the planner also serves another function. Instead of observing human problem-solving behavior, the learning element observes solutions generated by the performance element using more traditional weak methods (i.e., search). This allows the system to function as a closed loop: it provides its own observed problem-solving episodes, often generated at great computational expense, from which it learns new schemata. These new schemata then permit the system to solve similar problems at a far smaller computational expense. Note that for closed-loop systems, the entire structure generated by the performance element is handed over to the learning element: there is no need to reconstruct a causal model on the basis of the primitive operator sequence when the entire trace produced by the problem solver is available for use as a causal model.

3.4.2. The Learning Element

The learning element consists of two modules: the *understander*[11] and the *generalizer*. Input to the learning element consists of an *initial state*, a *goal state*, and an *observed sequence* of operators that transform

---

[10] The performance element is by no means the only benchmark for learning. It is quite possible to construct an explanation-based learning system with no performance element: learning in such a system would be demonstrated by its improved explanation-construction ability.

the former into the latter.

3.4.2.1. The Understander

The understander is the module that observes examples of problem-solving behavior. Its task is to construct a *causal model* of the observed input, from which a causally complete *explanation* of how the observed sequence accomplishes the goal state is derived.

The construction of the causal model involves the application of domain knowledge from the schema library. To do this, the understander must decide if a given schema from the schema library is *applicable* in the current context. The applicability of a given schema is determined by checking that schema's *application conditions*.

The reader should note that as the number of schemata in the schema library increases, the selection of relevant schemata and the checking of their application conditions holds the potential for combinatorial explosion. This is often referred to as the *schema* (or *frame) selection problem*. Avoiding this combinatorial pitfall is the subject of much work in AI [37, 40-42]. The strategy chosen to address the selection problem in the understander is termed the *schema activation* procedure.

Once a particular schema is deemed applicable, an *instance* of the schema is added to the causal model under construction. During this *instantiation* process a copy of the abstract schema from the schema library has its slots filled and is then connected, using appropriate links, with the rest of the causal model.

3.4.2.2. The Generalizer

The generalizer takes as its input the causal model constructed by the understander and produces a new schema. Before learning can take place, an explanation must be derived from the newly constructed causal model. Since an explanation is defined with respect to the goal that it accomplishes, some goal must be chosen with which to derive the

---

[11] Apologies to McDermott:

> We should avoid, for example, labeling any part of our programs an "understander." It is the job of the text accompanying the program to examine carefully how much understanding is present, how it got there, and what its limits are [8].

In this case, the alternate terms *justification analyzer* or *causal model builder*, while perhaps more acceptable from McDermott's point of view, conflict with our goal of descriptive simplicity. We choose to stick to the simpler, more intuitive terminology even at the risk of fooling ourselves.

explanation. In the PEBLS system of Figure 3.1, the goal is initially specified by the expert. In some domains it may be practical to specify a set of general goals so that no explicit goal specification need take place: the generalizer simply looks for instances of this goal set that are valid during the course of the observed episode and uses these instances as goals.

Given a goal and a causal model, the first step is to *verify* that the observed episode achieves the specified goal. It is the verification process that requires application of the domain theory. The crucial step of the verification process is the determination of which parts of the causal model contribute to the realization of the specified goal.

Once the goal has been verified, the generalizer must determine if it is worthwhile learning from the episode in question; i.e., whether it meets the *learning criteria*.

If the learning criteria are met, the generalizer may proceed to extract an explanation from the causal model, using relevance cues determined during the verification process. The generalizer can now proceed to build the new schema. Note that if the generalizer has more than one goal, these can be treated orthogonally, and thus several explanations may be derived from a single causal model. In these cases, more than one explanation may imply more than one new schema. This may be practical for those domains where the expert does not explicitly specify the goal.

Given the explanation, the generalizer now builds a new schema. There are three different strategies available for the generalizer:

(1) *Generalization* describes the process that takes an explanation derived from a particular instance of problem-solving behavior and yields a new schema that is a more abstract version of the explanation. The assumption is that the new more abstract schema will be applicable to situations other than the original observed situation. The actual process used differs substantially from system to system, but it is important that the explanation somehow be used to guide the construction of the new schema.

(2) *Specialization* describes the process where a more constrained version of a known schema is constructed and added to the schema library. It is important that the explanation be used to impose constraints on the more general schema to produce a useful addition to the library. A useful addition is usually one that can be applied with less effort by the performance element than the originally known schema, thus producing a gain in efficiency. Note, however, that the new schema is still subsumed by the more general, pre-existing, schema.

(3) *Refinement* refers to the process where a known schema is modified and replaced in the schema library. Such modification is based on the explanation constructed by the understander using the original schema. Note that, unlike specialization, the new schema is not subsumed by the original schema.

The generalizer must build more than just the new schema: each schema must also have a set of application conditions for use by the understander, as well as indexing pointers for use by the planner. Construction of a new schema requires establishing these sets of conditions, while refinement considers modifying an existing schema's application conditions.

If the newly generated schema meets the *retention criteria*, then it is integrated with extant schemata in the schema library. The new schema is now available for use by the performance element as well as by the understanding element when constructing other explanations. Continued use of the system would result in monotonic growth of the schema library. To keep the library at a manageable size, *replacement criteria* might be used in order to determine which existing schema is replaced by the new entry.

3.5. Issues for EBL Systems

There are several questions that can be asked about explanation-based systems that can help us to distinguish between the various approaches embodied in each different implementation, They are

(1) *Does the system build the explanation?* The explanation could be built by the understander, or, if it is a closed-loop system, the explanation can be a by-product of the performance element's search behavior. Alternatively, some systems require that the explanation be built by the teacher and input in its entirety. ARMS costructs its own explanations using a novel nonpredictive understanding process (see Section 5.3.1).

(2) *How does the system do explanation-based learning?* Does the system use generalization, specialization, and/or refinement? The ARMS system uses some form of specialization (see Section 5.3.2.1.2) as well as generalization (see Section 5.3.2.3).

(3) *What are the learning criteria?* Are all problem-solving inputs eventually passed to the generalizer? The ARMS learning criterion states that any example not initially analyzable by the system is worth learning from (see Section 5.3.2.1).

(4)   *Does the system acquire new schemata?* How does this learning process rely on the explanation? ARMS acquires new schemata by generalizing the explanation (see Sections 5.3.2.2. and 5.3.2.3).

(5)   *What are the retention criteria?* Is every new schema produced by the generalizer retained? ARMS retains everything it learns (see Section 5.3.2.4).

(6)   *Does the system learn application conditions?* Does the system *refine* the application conditions of existing schemata? ARMS learns application conditions (Section 5.3.2.5) but does not perform any form of schema refinement.

(7)   *Does the system perform unguided search in learning?* The use of unguided search in learning is not the same as doing search in the performance element. If the system is a closed-loop system, the performance element may very well do search in generating new problem-solving episodes. This is an orthogonal issue and should not be confused with the use of search in the learning process. ARMS is an open-loop system that does not perform any unguided search in learning.

(8)   *Does the system make the closed-world assumption?* The closed-world assumption holds that if the proposition P cannot be proven to hold true then the NOT(P) must be true. The ARMS implementation does not rely on the closed-world assumption (see Section 8.1.1).

(9)   *Does the system make the STRIPS assumption?* The STRIPS assumption holds that all operators change none of the program's beliefs except those explicitly listed in the operator description. The ARMS implementation does not rely on the STRIPS assumption (see Section 8.1.1).

Chapter 4
The Arms World

The ARMS system is an open-loop, explanation-based learning system with an architecture very much like that of the PEBLS system. It has two main components: a learning element and a performance element. Both of these components manipulate, through a symbolic representation stored in the database, some problem-solving domain (see Figure 4.1). In Chapter 5, we discuss the symbolic representation and the learning and performance elements; but first, in this chapter, we describe the problem-solving domain.

Ideally, this domain should consist of real-world pieces in a real-world workspace being moved around by a real-world robot arm. As one might expect, this approach entails solving a great number of equally real engineering problems, that, albeit interesting in their own right, are not terribly relevant to AI or machine learning.[12]

In order to sidestep these engineering problems, a program was written to simulate a robot arm moving through a simulated workspace. In this fashion, many of the hard engineering problems (arm control, kinematics, sensors, path planning, tolerances, etc.) are avoided,

---

[12] The current ARMS implementation was used to drive a MicroBot Teachmover(tm) five degree of freedom robot arm with moderate success. One immediate problem was due to the low accuracy and repeatability of this inexpensive hobbyist robot arm: a problem exacerbated by the workspace state uncertainty problem discussed in Chapter 8. This difficulty notwithstanding, the experience was, over all, encouraging. Many problems were due to the missing sixth degree of freedom: the ARMS primitive robot arm command set assumes the real robot arm has at least six degrees of freedom. [43] presents a detailed discussion of this real-world experiment, the problems encountered, and a local planning system devised to map the ARMS primitive robot arm command set onto the five degrees of freedom arm.

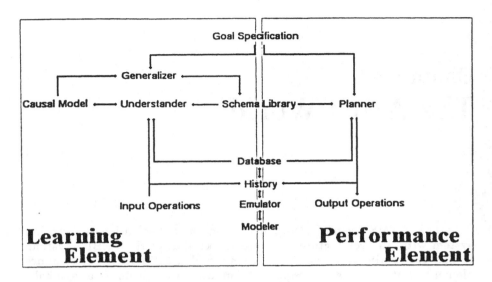

The ARMS Architecture

Figure 4.1

allowing us to concentrate on machine-learning issues. Using this approach, the translation from the simulated world into the internal representation is not subject to sensor problems, in effect creating the perfect sensory system with complete knowledge of the real (emulated) world.

We begin our discussion with a description of the idealized simulated world. We then describe the structure of the simulation program and its logical subdivision into a *modeler*, an *emulator*, and a *history mechanism*.

4.1. Characterizing the Robot World

We can characterize the idealized robot world by describing its *physical components* and a *domain theory*. The three physical components of the idealized world are

(1)   a collection of *pieces*, some of which are used in the assembly;

(2)   a *workspace* that provides a surface on which the pieces may rest; and

(3) a *robot arm*, capable of moving about the workspace and manipulating the pieces.

4.1.1. The Pieces

A piece is a rigid solid object that has no moving parts. A piece is always *supported* by another piece, the workspace, or (when being held) by the robot arm. In our idealized world, each piece has one and only one supporter, although a piece or the workspace may support more than one other piece.

Different pieces can be combined to form *assemblies* by inserting parts of one piece into holes on another. Depending on the relative sizes and shapes of the inserted portions, these assemblies exhibit different mechanical behaviors. This behavior is described by the *domain theory* described below in Section 4.1.4.

4.1.2. The Workspace

The workspace is little more than a table top on which the pieces may rest. It may support any number of pieces, which in turn may support yet other pieces stacked on top of them.

4.1.3. The Robot Arm

The robot arm is a positioning device that can place its *end effector* at any location and orientation within its *workspace envelope*. The end effector in the ARMS domain consists of a *palm* and two *fingers* configured as a *gripper*. The position of the gripper is measured at the point (called the *hot spot*) that lies directly between the two fingers (see Figure 4.2).

As mentioned briefly in Chapter 2, the robot arm responds to the following five *primitive robot arm commands*:

(1) *Open:* Open the gripper fingers to their maximum aperture.

(2) *Close:* Close the gripper fingers as far as possible, stopping when they meet or when any intervening piece obstructs further movement.

(3) *Translate (unitVector, delta):* Move the gripper from its present position in a straight line along the given axis by delta units while maintaining the orientation of the gripper (see Figure 4.3).

(4) *Rotate (unitVector, theta):* Rotate the gripper about the given axis by theta degrees while maintaining the current location of the gripper (see Figure 4.4).

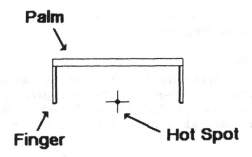

ARMS Gripper

Figure 4.2

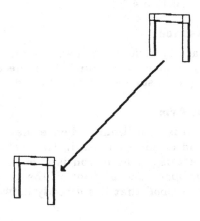

Translate (unitVector, delta)

Figure 4.3

Rotate (unitVector, delta)

Figure 4.4

(5) *MoveTo (newPosition):* Move the gripper from its current position
to newPosition along any collision-free path. Note that newPosition
specifies both the location and orientation of the gripper hot spot
(see Figure 4.5).

While this command set is not that of any particular industrial
robot arm, it is fairly representative. Note that nearly any arm
possessing the minimum requisite degrees of freedom (six plus gripper)
can be made to implement these five commands, at least within some
restricted workspace envelope.

The implementations of the gripper commands Open and Close on
a real robot arm are quite straightforward, since neither one of these
commands requires changing the position of the arm in space. The other

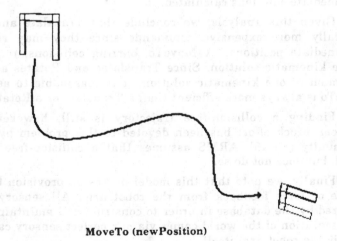

MoveTo (newPosition)

Figure 4.5

three commands, however, entail repositioning the gripper, and therefore, their implementations require computing an arm trajectory.

Computing a trajectory for a robot arm implies

(1)   finding a path through space for the gripper, the arm linkages, and any object being held by the gripper such that collisions are avoided, and

(2)   calculating the motor control voltages necessary to move the gripper along this path.

For a given robot arm geometry, the kinematics of this control problem are well understood [44]. Solving the kinematic formulae for a given trajectory is fairly straightforward, albeit computationally intensive.

If there are no obstacles to avoid, a MoveTo requires a single kinematic solution. Each motor is then servoed to its final position, resulting in an uneven path as measured at the end effector. This type of movement is termed *joint interpolated motion* in the robotics literature.

To produce smooth motion, such as that required by a Translate or Rotate, intermediate kinematic solutions must be computed. Each motor is servoed to successive intermediate positions. Note that the cost of computing the kinematic solution grows with the number of intermediate solutions calculated.

Given this analysis, we conclude that Translate and Rotate are generally more expensive commands since they may require many intermediate positions. A MoveTo, barring collisions, requires only a single kinematic solution. Since Translates and Rotates also require a minimum of one kinematic solution, it is reasonable to assume that a MoveTo is always more efficient than a Translate or a Rotate.

Finding a collision-free trajectory is still, however, a difficult problem. Much effort has been devoted to this problem by the robotics community [45, 46]: ARMS assumes that a collision-free path can be found, but does not do so.

Finally, we note that this model makes no provision for the use of tactile or force feedback from the robot arm. All sensory information required by the database in order to construct and maintain its symbolic representation of the world comes via our perfect sensory capability, and not via the robot arm itself.

4.1.4. The Robot World Domain Theory

The domain theory is a naive kinematic theory that attempts to account for relative piece motions. It describes the aggregate behavior of individual pieces when they are put together into assemblies. It is loosely based on [47].

We define a *link* to be a rigid solid body, with an arbitrary number of Cartesian coordinate systems, or *hooks*, affixed to the solid to serve as reference points. A *joint* relates two links by specifying a hook from each link together with a parameterized *transform* giving the legal relative positions between hooks.

The number of independent variables in the transform indicates the number of *degrees of freedom* in the joint. A degree of freedom describes one type of allowed motion. It may be either *prismatic* or *revolute*, and must give both upper and lower limits for the motion it allows. Two unrelated (and therefore unconstrained) pieces have six degrees of freedom between them: three revolute and three prismatic. The prismatic degrees of freedom are all orthogonal, as are the revolute ones. Two rigidly constrained bodies have zero degrees of freedom between them.

We can construct a *taxonomy of joints* based on the degrees of freedom they allow. Some of the common joint types are

RigidJoint - zero degrees of freedom.
PrismaticJoint - one prismatic degree of freedom.
RevoluteJoint - one revolute degree of freedom.
CylindricalJoint - one revolute and one prismatic degree of freedom.
UniversalJoint - two revolute degrees of freedom.
SphericalJoint - three revolute degrees of freedom.
NullJoint - all six degrees of freedom.

It is important to realize that there are only a finite number of combinations of degrees of freedom possible, and, therefore, only a finite number of joint types. However, there may be many different ways to physically implement a particular joint.

Each degree of freedom has a *range* that indicates the values the corresponding variable may assume. The range is bounded on both sides by one of two types of bounds:

(1) A *hard bound* corresponds to a physical limit imposed by the mechanism. Such a bound occurs when two surfaces collide. For example, imagine a square tab sliding back and forth in a slot: a hard bound on either end limits its travel.

(2) A *soft bound* corresponds to a limit that may be physically exceeded by the mechanism, but if exceeded will cause the joint to

fail. A soft bound would occur when the tab mentioned above is pulled straight out from the slot.

An *open kinematic chain* is a transitive relation between two pieces not directly related in a single joint. Such a chain may span two or more simple joints to form a *composite joint*. For example, consider the widget of Chapter 2. The widget can be characterized as a revolute joint between the washer and the block. Closer examination, however, reveals that this revolute joint is a combination of two subjoints: a cylindrical joint between the washer and the peg, and a rigid joint between the peg and the block.

4.2. Simulating the Robot World

The computer program that simulates the ARMS world can be divided, for the purpose of this discussion, into three convenient elements.

(1)   The *solid modeler* is used to represent the state of the world at any given time.

(2)   The *emulator* takes a world snapshot and a robot arm command and computes a new, updated, snapshot of the world illustrating the effects of the executed arm command.

(3)   The *history mechanism* maintains and indexes each of the workspace snapshots, permitting complete access to each world state over time.

4.2.1. The Solid Modeler

In this section we describe the solid modeler and how it is used to represent the world state at a given time. The modeler provides a means for representing static snapshots of the ARMS domain. Each of the three physical components of the idealized robot world (pieces, robot arm, and workspace) is represented in a *solid modeling* paradigm. The modeler supports certain static relations between these components, such as determining what each piece is resting on. In addition, the modeler provides for graphic display of the current state of the domain.

The ARMS modeler is a simplified hybrid modeler: a cross between a *constructive solid geometry* (CSG) and a *boundary representation* (BRep).[13] The system supports two *primitives*, the *block* and the *right cylinder*. Instances of these primitives, of varying dimensions, are put together with CSG *combination operators* to produce *pieces*. Only two

---

[13] For a review of constructive solid geometries and a description of the terms used in describing the ARMS modeler, see Appendix A.

combination operators are supported:

(1) The *disjoint-union* operator joins two primitives surface-to-surface. This is a restricted form of the general union operator where the primitive pieces must abut with no volume overlap (see Figure 4.6). One can think of this operator as adding a solid primitive onto another, abutting, solid primitive.

(2) The *contained-difference* operator removes one primitive from another. The primitive being removed must share at least one surface with the larger primitive, and its volume must be totally contained in the larger primitive (see Figure 4.7). This is also a restricted form of the general difference operator. One can think of this operator as removing a nonsolid primitive from a different (solid) primitive with a shared surface.

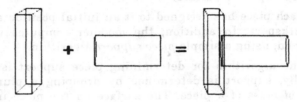

Disjoint Union Operator

Figure 4.6

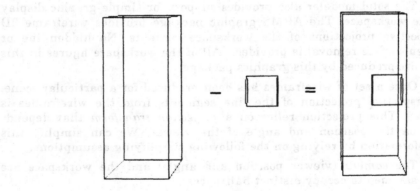

Contained Difference Operator

Figure 4.7

Restricting the modeler to these two operators simplifies the CSG to BRep conversion. As the CSG combination operators are used to specify pieces, the pieces' BRep surface set is constructed by simple manipulations of its constituent primitives' surface sets. For the block, these are the six rectangular *planar surfaces*. For the cylinder, there are two round planar surfaces and a single exterior *cylindrical surface*. We thus replace the potentially expensive CSG to BRep conversion algorithm with a simple filter function that operates on the union of surface sets of the constituent primitives (see Section 6.4.1.4).

Once the pieces are created, they are added to a new static model of the ARMS domain. This static model, called a *workspace model*, contains pointers to modelers' representations of every piece in the workspace, the model of the robot arm, and the representation of the table top (a planar surface).

Each piece has assigned to it an initial position and orientation in the workspace. In addition, the modeler computes what the piece is resting on, using a simple *piece support* algorithm.

The algorithm for determining piece support is somewhat naive. Basically, support is determined by dropping a plumb line from the center of mass of a piece. The surface on the piece intersected by this plumb line which is furthest from the center of mass is the *support surface*. Support is provided by the *supporting surface* in contact with the support surface that also intersects the plumb line.

The solid modeler also provides support for simple graphic display of the workspace. The ARMS graphic package provides wireframe 3D perspective projections of the workspace contents. No hidden-line or hidden-surface removal is provided. All of the workspace figures in this book are produced by this graphics package.

Once a set of wireframes has been produced for a particular scene, a perspective projection of the line segments from the wireframes is created. This projection relies on a *projection transform* that depends only on the position and angle of the viewer. We can simplify this transformation by relying on the following simplifying assumptions:

(1) The *camera* (viewer position and angle) and the workspace are assumed to occupy distinct halfspaces.

(2) The plane separating the two halfspaces is the *projection plane*; e.g., analogous to the screen in a movie theater (Figure 4.8).

The first assumption eliminates the need for a clipping algorithm. This reduces the computational costs of projecting the image onto the projection plane. The disadvantage is that the camera cannot be moved behind or over the workspace to get a different view of the action.

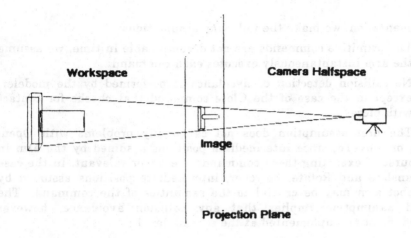

Projection Halfspaces

Figure 4.8

The second assumption simplifies the mathematics and increases the efficiency of the graphics package by reducing the number of matrix calculations. On the other hand, the disadvantage is that as the camera moves away from a centered position, the image becomes more and more distorted. Just as in a movie theater, it is best to sit in the center seats, and not on either side.

4.2.2. The Emulator

Given the workspace snapshot Wt at time t, and a robot arm command, the emulator constructs the next workspace snapshot $Wt+1$. Note that the emulator's task definition presupposes a notion of time: ARMS employs a simple temporal model that assigns a single unit of time, or a *tick*, to every robot arm command. Given this task description, we can divide the emulator's job into two subtasks: computing the effects of the robot arm command on the robot arm, and computing any side effects of the arm's motion on the pieces in the workspace.

4.2.2.1. Moving the Robot Arm

In Section 4.1.4, we described the command set for the idealized ARMS robot arm. For each of the commands, we implement a procedure that computes the new position and orientation of the arm from its current state and the command parameters. In order to simplify the implementation, we make the following assumptions:

(1)   The primitive commands are not decomposable in time: we assume the arm instantaneously executes each command.

(2)   No collision detection or avoidance is performed by the modeler, except in the case of the Close command that checks for contact with pieces.

The first assumption does not cause any problems with Open, Close, or MoveTo, since intermediate positions assumed by the arm in the course of executing these commands are never relevant. In the case of Translate and Rotate, however, intermediate positions assumed by the robot arm may be crucial to the semantics of the command. The second assumption implies that any collision avoidance, however limited, must be implemented at the schema level.

4.2.2.2. Modeling Robot/Piece Interactions

The only robot/piece interaction supported by the emulator occurs when the robot arm is used to grasp and move a piece. We make the following simplifying assumptions:

(1)   The arm can manipulate only one piece at a time.

(2)   A piece cannot be manipulated if it is providing support for any other piece in the workspace.

(3)   Contact between the gripper and a piece is assumed to be perfect: the piece is never allowed to slip while being held between the fingers.

(4)   The gripper contacts are modeled as two points, one on the end of each finger. For a finger to be in contact with the surface of a piece, it is sufficient for the contact point to be on the surface.

(5)   A piece can only be grasped by opposing surfaces that belong to the same CSG primitive. As an illustration, consider the illegal grasping strategy shown in Figure 4.9. Note that the two contact surfaces belong to two different CSG primitives.

(6)   When a piece is dropped by the robot arm, it must receive support from either another piece or the workspace itself.

The first two assumptions together prohibit the robot from moving, for example, a stack of blocks. This assumption could conceivably be relaxed a bit in order to allow the robot arm to manipulate, under certain constraints, all of the pieces that belong to the same mechanism at once. This would allow the arm to move the entire widget assembly of Chapter 2 as a unit.

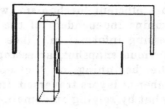

Example of Illegal Grasping Strategy

Figure 4.9

The purpose of the third assumption, and of the first two as well, is to keep any uncertainty in piece position from creeping into the system. Such uncertainty might occur when moving an unstable stack of blocks. Another possible source of uncertainty is for a piece to slip while being carried by the gripper.

The last three assumptions are the least restrictive, and are imposed only to simplify implementation of the solid modeler.

As with collision avoidance, any other type of robot/piece interactions must be implemented at the schema level. For example, neither the modeler nor the emulator enforce collision avoidance between the arm and a piece in the workspace, but the schema level representation provides some minimal collision avoidance behavior when approaching a piece for grasping.

4.2.3. The History Mechanism

The history mechanism manages the workspace snapshots produced by the emulator. A naive implementation would be to make a new copy of the workspace snapshot at each time tick. Although simple to implement, this kind of strategy is extremely costly in terms of storage. In fact, the cost of a new copy grows with the number of pieces in the workspace.

A more storage-efficient history mechanism can be implemented once one notices that most of the information contained in the snapshot is invariant from one time tick to the next: e.g., piece sizes/shapes do not change, only a single piece is manipulated at a time, and once a piece has been put somewhere, it is likely to stay there for a while. Thus each successive snapshot records only the changes made from the preceding snapshot.

By using this more efficient mechanism, we see that the cost for each new snapshot remains independent of the size of the workspace. The tradeoff is in accessing information. Since each snapshot forms a new layer over the previous snapshot, accessing information that has not changed since the beginning of the episode will take time proportional to the number of layers traversed. In practice, this behavior can be improved somewhat by relying on domain-specific traits.

In summary, when properly implemented, this history mechanism is totally transparent: the rest of the system accesses what appear to be distinct snapshots of each world state. There is, of course, some slight increase in the access time for certain information that increases linearly with the number of snapshots. The storage requirements are vastly reduced when compared to the naive approach. For implementation details, see Section 6.4.3.

Chapter 5
Learning And Problem Solving

From a machine-learning perspective, the most interesting aspects of the ARMS system are in the learning and performance elements. Recall that ARMS is an open-loop, explanation-based learning system (see Figure 5.1), with learning and performance elements accessing a symbolic representation of the world stored in the database.

We begin this chapter with a discussion of the symbolic representation manipulated by the learning and performance elements, as well as the database mechanism that maintains it. Next, we discuss the performance element and how it applies extant schemata to achieve a given goal specification. Finally, we examine the learning element and how it acquires new schemata by observing an expert's solution to a given problem.

5.1. Knowledge Representation

In this section we describe the ARMS schema system.[14] Recall that the ARMS learning and performance elements do not directly access the real world, but rather shuttle all queries for world information through a database system. The database system contains data structures, called *schemata*, that represent relations and events in the world. We begin with a description of schema structure, and then discuss the database system.

_____

[14] Appendix B contains a review of some of the more common terminology used in describing schema-based knowledge representation systems. Appendix F contains a capsule summary of the schemata initially built into the ARMS system.

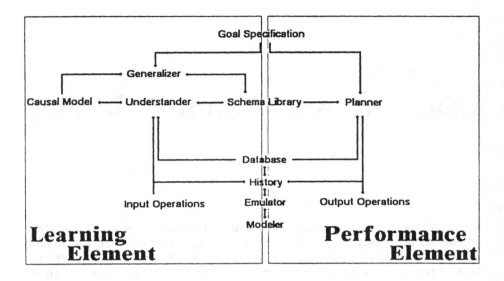

The ARMS Architecture

Figure 5.1

5.1.1. The Schema System

We divide ARMS schemata into two main categories: *state schemata* that are used to describe relations in the world, and *operator schemata* that describe operations that can be applied to the world. The relations expressed by state schemata as well as the operations represented by operator schemata often refer to physical objects in the ARMS world. These physical objects are represented by *descriptors*, that are elements of the solid modeling system (see Section 4.2.1).

Implicit in the division of operator vs. state schemata is a naive temporal model. This model assumes that state schema instances may be valid over a period of time, while those operator schema instances corresponding to the primitive robot arm commands are considered to be instantaneous. This is an adequate temporal model given that there is only one active agent in the ARMS domain (the robot arm).

5.1.1.1. State Schemata

A state schema is a *partial description* of the domain. It permits the system to assert that one particular relation is valid at a given time.

For example, given the initial state of the training example (see Figure 2.2), it is possible to assert a state schema which corresponds to "$Peg1 is stacked on top of $Washer1."

Every state schema has two time slots: a *start time* that gives an integer representing the first clock tick where this particular instance is valid, and an *end time* that gives an integer representing the last clock tick where this particular instance is valid.

The validity of a particular state schema at a given time must be determined independently by examining the domain. There are, however, a couple of special slots on each state schema that can help confirm the validity of a particular state schema instance.

(1) A state schema may contain a set of schema templates on a *substantiator* slot. These state schema templates indicate other state schemata that must be valid for this state to also be valid. Validity of all of these state schemata is a necessary, but not sufficient, condition for validity of the original state schema. This can be useful if the expense associated in validating the substantiator is less than that associated with validating the given state schema itself.

(2) A state schema may contain a set of schema templates on a *contradictions* slot. These state schema templates indicate other state schemata that, if valid, invalidate the current state. As before, not being able to validate any of the contradictions is a necessary, but not sufficient, condition for validity of the original state schema. Again, this can be useful if the expense associated in attempting to validate the contradiction is less than that associated with validating the given state schema.

(3) A state schema may contain a set of constraint schema templates (described below) on a *constraints* slot. These constraint schema templates serve to limit what fillers the slots of the state schema may assume.

There are two special subclasses of state schemata: *constraint schemata* and *joint schemata*.

5.1.1.1.1. Constraint Schemata

A constraint schema is a special type of state schema used to represent a temporally fixed relationship in the world. Because of this time invariance, constraint schemata may be treated in a slightly more efficient fashion by the state database.

A constraint schema contains the special slots Type, Path1, Path2, and Constant. The Type slot represents some relation that, if true when evaluated with the other arguments of the schema, determines the validity of the entire schema. The relation may be either unary or binary. Path1 and Path2 represent pointers (or paths of pointers) to particular slots in the state schema to whom this particular constraint belongs. Constant contains a pointer to a constant. In the case of a unary Type, Path1 provides the argument. For a binary Type, Path2 or Constant provides the second argument: hence they must never co-occur.

For example, given a schema $A with slot X, we can constrain X to have a numeric filler with value less than 5 for all instances Ai$ of $A. We do this by listing the following constraint schema templates on the Constraints slot of $A:

```
($ConstraintSchema (Type NUMBERP)
                   (Path1 :X))
```

```
($ConstraintSchema (Type LESSP)
                   (Path1 :X)
                   (Constant 5))
```

5.1.1.1.2. Joint Schemata

A joint schema is a special type of state schema used to implement the ARMS domain theory (see Section 4.1.5). It represents the motion allowed between two pieces in the workspace. In our implementation, joints are defined between primitives belonging to two different pieces. They can be characterized by their constituent degrees of freedom.

We divide joint schemata into two distinct types:

(1) *Abstract joint schemata* contain knowledge that describes the mechanical behavior of a joint in terms of its degrees of freedom. These schemata are pre-encoded into the system. While ARMS does not contain a full set of these schemata, given that only a finite number of degrees of freedom exist between two pieces, only a finite number of abstract joint schemata need be built in.

(2) *Physical joint schemata* contain information about the physical implementation of the desired abstract joint behavior. Some of these schemata are also pre-encoded in the ARMS system, but others (e.g., $RevoluteJointA) are acquired automatically by the system during the goal verification step (see Section 5.3.2.1.2).

For example, consider the widget described in Chapter 2. We encode knowledge about the expected function of the joint in the abstract joint schema $RevoluteJoint. This knowledge indicates that the joint will permit one revolute degree of freedom between the two base pieces of the assembly. But this tells us nothing about *how* the assembly is put together.

In fact, in the widget example, the physical realization of $RevoluteJoint required achieving first a $CylindricalJoint (two degrees of freedom, one revolute and one prismatic, between the peg and the washer) and then constraining the prismatic degree of freedom with a $RigidJoint between the peg and the block. An analysis of the assembly indicates the existence of an open kinematic chain between the block and the washer (via the peg) which contains only the remaining revolute degree of freedom.

Knowledge about how the joint is realized is stored in the physical joint schema $RevoluteJointA. This schema tells us one way of implementing the functional behavior described in the abstract joint schema $RevoluteJoint. Note that $RevoluteJoint relates only the two base pieces, while $RevoluteJointA must mention the third piece involved in the assembly.

The abstract joint schema indexes those physical joint schemata that represent their known consistent physical implementations. Hence, $RevoluteJoint points to all known physical implementations of its function, including, of course, $RevoluteJointA. From a given instantiation of an abstract joint schema, we can derive a set of instantiations for possible physical implementations of the abstract joint. Constraints attached to physical joint schemata are used to represent the physical features as well as physical interdependencies of various pieces used in the assembly.

There are three specific assumptions about the ARMS domain that simplify the implementation of the domain theory:

(1) Joints arise from interactions between CSG primitives rather than CSG surfaces. This limits the number of joint types that must be built into the system, and places greater reliance on composite joints for representing complex mechanisms.

(2) Degrees of freedom are always considered independently of one another, hence, the value of each joint variable is an independent variable. This means that a screw joint, which has dependent prismatic and revolute degrees of freedom, cannot be represented in this implementation.

(3) Similarly, boundary conditions for each degree of freedom are also calculated independently. This means that, for example, the maximum travel of a sliding piece cannot depend on the value of another joint variable.

A more complete domain theory would recognize that some degrees of freedom are interdependent; that their boundary conditions may depend on the current value of a different degree of freedom. In addition, a more complete domain theory should permit modeling of joints based on surface interactions. In such a theory, any surface contact (such as stacking one block on another) would result in some limitation of interpiece movement.

5.1.1.2. Operator Schemata

An operator schema represents an operation or a set of operations on the world that result in changes to the state description. Five of the operator schemata in ARMS represent the *primitive operator schemata*. The rest of the operator schemata correspond to *composites* of other operator schemata.

In general, every operator schema contains (at least) the following slots:

(1) A set of *goals* that are state schema templates for schemata achieved by executing the operation(s) represented by this schema. The set need not be exhaustive; thus, an operator may have unknown side effects.

(2) A set of *preconditions* that are state schema templates for schemata that must be valid to execute the operation(s) represented by this operator schema.

(3) A set of *subgoals*, that are state schema templates. The state schemata indicated by the subgoals are represented as schema templates in a causally ordered structure, the *subgoal poset*. Templates at the same list level are causally dependent and must always occur temporally in the given order. Templates at embedded levels are causally independent and can occur in any temporal ordering. For example, the subgoal poset:

[($A (X Y))($B (X Y)(W Z)) [($C (X Y))($D (Z W))]]

indicates that an instance of $A must be achieved before an instance of $B, which must in turn be achieved before instances of $C and $D, although the last two may be achieved in either order.

(4) A single operator schema template called the *body* that represents a (different) operation. When executed in the context established by achieving the subgoals in a world where all of the preconditions are valid, the body will achieve the goals of this operator schema.

(5) A set of operator schema templates called *suggestions* that are usually templates for each schema having this schema as its body. Under certain conditions, new schemata produced by the generalizer may not adhere to this convention (see Section 5.3.2.5).

Instances of primitive operator schemata also have a *time slot* that gives the clock tick at which this particular schema instance was applied to the world. Note that primitive operator schemata have no body (they are directly executable), no subgoals (they cannot be broken down any further), and no preconditions (every arm command is always executable).

Using this description, it is possible to layer instances of operator schemata into some sort of graph, that bottoms out at the level of primitive operators. Building this structure bottom-up is precisely how causal models (from which explanations are extracted) are constructed. The corresponding top-down expansion of such structures forms the basis for the performance element.

5.1.2. The Database Mechanism

The symbolic representation used by ARMS relies on state schemata to represent physical relations that are true at the modeler and emulator levels. The database mechanism is used to hold the state schemata that describe past and current world states. Every request by the performance or learning elements for information about the world state must be routed through this mechanism.

What form do these requests take? In its simplest form, a request consists of an instantiated (all parameters bound) state schema that the database must compare against the current world model to return a verdict: either the relation described by this state schema holds or it does not.

But not all requests are this straightforward: a request may be only partially specified. This is the case when certain slots of the schema are not yet bound. In this case, the database must return a list of all valid (fully instantiated) state schemata which match this partially instantiated request. These state schemata should be *unique*, in the sense that for every relation that holds true at some time in the system, there is only one, unique, state schema which represents it.

Finally, the database must be able to represent relations as they change with time. Requests from the understander may not always pertain to the current world state: the understander may need to know if a certain relation was true at some previous time. From the database's point of view, the emulator level appears to retain a set of copies of the world model at each time tick. The database must therefore use the same state schema to represent a relation that persists across several snapshots.

In the sections that follow, we describe some of the aspects of the database mechanism.

5.1.2.1. State Schema Validation

Every state schema built into the ARMS system has a procedure, called a *validation procedure*, that can be used to ascertain the validity of an instance of the state at a given tick. This procedure usually entails some form of geometric reasoning. The exact procedure used to validate a given state varies for each state type. For example, if the state schema request were "is $Peg1 stacked on $Block1 at time t?" it is sufficient to go to the world snapshot[15] for time t and check the relative positions of $Peg1 and $Block1, surfaces in contact, and so on.

The validation procedure is responsible for fleshing out the slots of partially instantiated requests. In the case of multiple consistent instantiations, the schema is split into multiple copies, or *clones*, that differ in the previously unfilled slots. For example, if the request were "is something stacked on $Block1 at time t?" and there were two pieces stacked on $Block1, the validation procedure would return two distinct state schemata, one for each valid stacked relation.

Many of the validation procedures are computationally expensive. Much of the expense is due to filling out the unfilled slots. For this reason, there is a simpler procedure for extending the validity of a state schema valid at time t to time $t+1$ or t-1. This simpler procedure, called a *confirmation procedure*, attempts to extend the validity of a previously validated state schema. For example, in the stacking example given above, it is sufficient to ascertain that neither piece has changed position.

5.1.2.2. Caching Valid State Schema Instances

Considering the computational expense involved in validating a state schema, we would like to avoid validating the same relation more than once. It is common for a same relation to occur as a precondition or subgoal of many different operators. For example, the same grasped relation may serve as a precondition for several operator schemata.

For this reason, it makes good sense to cache those state schemata found to be valid. Since there must be a unique state schema for a given relation, future requests must first be compared to these known valid schemata. If a valid schema which matches the request can be found in the cache, no validation need be performed. At worst, there may be some work involved in extending the temporal scope of the cached state to match the request. Note that any caching strategy

---

[15] Recall from our discussion of Section 4.2.3 we will consider the history mechanism to be transparent: hence we will refer to "world snapshots at time t" instead of "history mechanism layer at time t."

entails some sort of matching mechanism that can determine if two state schema instances represent the same thing.

Special attention must be paid to the temporal extension process: a given request at two different ticks must return the same state schema if and only if the validity of the state is not compromised at any intermediate tick. If this is not the case, then two separate state schemata should be returned. For example, if $Peg1 is stacked on top of $Block1, then removed and later replaced, there should be two different stacked states representing these two separate stacking events.

One must be careful not to confuse the caching mechanism with the history mechanism of Section 4.2.3. The history mechanism permits temporal layering of the numerically emulated world, where each layer differs from the previous layer in precisely those items changed by the arm command for that tick. The caching mechanism uniquely identifies and manages many symbolic partial representations of the world. Aside from obvious differences between the numerically emulated world and its symbolic representation, note that each partial symbolic representation, or state schema, may *persist* through time, therefore spanning multiple history snapshots.

5.1.2.3. Database Parallelism

Even though state schemata are checked against the emulator's world snapshots only as a result of a request, the amount of time spent by the database in satisfying these requests accounts for a large portion of the computational resources expended by the ARMS system.[16]

We note that validating these requests is, in a sense, a *read-only* operation. No changes are made to a world snapshot as a result of a validation or confirmation procedure. This fact makes this kind of database mechanism an ideal example of those algorithms best suited to large-grain-size parallel machines [48, 49].

Assuming that each processor can be given access to the world snapshots, each validation procedure could be run independently of the others. While ARMS runs on a serial machine, its object-oriented implementation (described in Chapter 6) makes explicit the inherently asynchronous aspect of the validation and confirmation operations.

---

[16] In fact, preliminary empirical evidence provided in Appendix E indicates that the database mechanism accounts for over 90% of the CPU time requirements for both learning and problem-solving episodes.

5.2. The Performance Element

In this section, we examine how schemata (both hand-encoded and acquired) are used by the system in the course of problem solving. A *problem-solving episode* is given by an *initial state* and a *goal specification*. The performance element yields a solution to the problem-solving episode in the form of an *output sequence* of primitive operators (robot arm commands) that transforms the initial state into a final state consistent with the goal specification.

The ARMS performance element consists of a *schema planner*, akin to the *skeletal planner* of [50]. It is a very simple design that begins by selecting an abstract plan to achieve the specified goal state, and then continues by recursively expanding the plan until the process bottoms out with a robot arm command sequence. The planning process is basically a depth-first search through the plan space defined by the schemata stored in the schema library.

We divide the planning process into two distinct phases: a *design phase* and a *planning phase*, which we describe in the following sections.

5.2.1. The Design Phase

The goal specification is given to the ARMS system as an abstract joint schema template. This serves as a functional description of the desired assembly. The object of the design phase is to produce, from this functional description, a physical description of the desired assembly. This is often called the *design problem*. It is in some sense the inverse of the *verification problem* of the learning element (see Section 5.3.2.1).

The goal specification is given as a partially instantiated abstract joint schema. The first step in the design phase is to flesh out the abstract joint goal schema by filling out the unfilled slots in accordance with the constraints on the schema. Constraints that pertain to interdependencies of the degrees of freedom are attached to the abstract joint schema. This is the abstract joint schema *realization* procedure. Note that the realization procedure may result in several possible instantiations of this abstract joint schema. All of the instantiations found are retained for possible backtracking. We continue the design phase with only one of the instantiated abstract joint schemata.

The abstract joint schema indexes those physical joint schemata which represent physical implementations consistent with this abstract joint. Thus from a given instantiation of an abstract joint schema, we can derive a set of instantiated physical joint schemata. These physical joint schemata are usually only partially instantiated as well: they too must have their unfilled slots fleshed out in accordance with the constraints they bear. Constraints attached to physical joint schemata are used to represent the physical features as well as interdependencies of various pieces used in the assembly.

As before, the realization process performed on a physical joint schema may result in multiple instantiations. These are also retained for possible backtracking. The planning phase receives only one of the instantiated physical joint schemata at a time, and, if there is a plan failure, an attempt is made to plan for the next physical joint schema.

If there is no known realizable implementation of the abstract joint goal schema, the planner quits and does not expend further effort attempting to search design space for a valid implementation. This is the case in the example of Chapter 2: the system had no previous knowledge of how to physically realize a revolute joint.

5.2.2. The Planning Phase

Given one of the fully instantiated physical joint schemata produced in the design phase, the planning phase attempts to produce a sequence of primitive robot arm commands that achieves it. The physical joint schemata resulting from the design phase can be thought of as a set of alternate goals, each of which is consistent with the goal specification supplied by the expert. If the system can achieve any one of these, the goal specification will be met.

Recall that all operator schemata in the schema library are indexed by the goals they achieve. Since physical joint schemata are state schemata, they too have pointers to operators that can achieve them. If the operator is a newly acquired schema, then the pointer will have just been added by the learning element. Finding an operator schema to achieve a given state schema is called the *plan step*.

In addition, it is possible that any given state schema may have multiple operator schemata that can serve as valid plans. Thus, from the given physical joint schema we can determine a set of operator schemata.

We instantiate the first element of the operator set and attempt to *execute* it. If the first operator is not executable, and no changes have been caused by its unsuccessful execution, we then attempt to execute the next instantiated operator. This process continues until one of the operators executes successfully, no operators remain, or some change is made to the world during an unsuccessful execution attempt.

Note that the plan step provides for only a limited form of backtracking. This is not a full depth-first search through the plan space, since backtracking may be aborted by an unsuccessful execution attempt.

The execution step for a given operator $X proceeds as follows:

(1) For every goal Gi$ of $X, query the state database to determine the validity of Gi$. If every Gi$ is valid, terminate execution successfully, returning $X. This is the case when the goals are all already established; thus, there is no need to execute the plan.

(2) For every precondition Pj$ of $X, query the state database to ascertain its validity at the current time. If any precondition is not currently valid, abort execution and return failure. Note that the preconditions may not have had all of their slots bound; therefore, this step may, by mapping values back via the template from the preconditions, create multiple consistent copies of $X. These are retained for possible backtracking.

(3) For every subgoal Sk$ of $X, query the state database to ascertain its validity at the current time. If a subgoal is not currently valid, attempt to recursively plan for the subgoal. If any subgoal is not valid and is not plannable, abort execution and return failure. As before, each of the subgoals must be realized, and any unfilled slots may result in multiple consistent copies of Sk$. Alternative instantiations may again cause, through mappings back across the template, multiple copies of $X to be retained for backtracking.

(4) Instantiate the body $B of $X and execute it recursively. Success or failure of this execution step is determined by the success or failure of the execution step of Bl$.

Note that if, at any time, an operator schema cannot be executed (due, for example, to unmet preconditions) or a state schema has no associated plans, the schema planner attempts to backtrack, and, failing that, simply quits. It does not waste effort attempting to sequentially combine operator schemata, an effort whose nature we know to be hopelessly combinatorial.

In summary, we divide the planning phase into repeated applications of two distinct steps:

(1) A *plan step*, that takes an instantiated state schema and generates a set of operator schemata, each corresponding to a plan for achieving the given state. The execution step is invoked on each of the resulting operator schemata in turn, until one of the execution steps terminates successfully. If none of the generated operator schemata is executed successfully, return failure.

(2) An *execution step*, that takes an operator schema, ascertains its preconditions are met, and then plans for each of its subgoals. If each subgoal is either currently valid or achieved by planning recursively, the execution step returns as its value the result of

attempting to execute the body of the operator recursively. Note that the execution step may clone copies of the operator schema for addition to the backtracking list of the plan step.

5.3. The Learning Element

A *learning episode* consists of an *initial state*, a *goal specification* (in terms of abstract joint schemata), and an *input sequence* of primitive operators (robot arm commands). The operator sequence, when executed by the robot arm in the context of the initial state, produces the *final state*.

As with PEBLS, the ARMS learning element consists of two modules: an *understander* and a *generalizer*. The purpose of the understander is to construct a *causal model* of the observed problem-solving behavior. The causal model is then analyzed by the generalizer, and new schemata are constructed. ARMS performs two types of explanation-based learning: *specialization* in the construction of new physical joint schemata, and *generalization* in the construction of new (macro) operator schemata. Both types of learning require a causal analysis of an explanation which relies on the domain theory.

5.3.1. The Understander

The *understander* takes as its inputs the initial state and the input sequence. It produces as its output a causal model of the external agent's problem-solving behavior. The causal model is then passed to the generalizer for analysis and possible learning.

5.3.1.1. Specifying the Initial State

The initial state is specified by the expert at the modeler level. A new workspace is created, and the expert specifies the pieces in it by giving their CSG descriptions and initial positions. The solid modeler checks the initial placement and determines what is supporting each piece in the workspace. A robot arm is then added to the new workspace. The initial placement of the arm is in the *nest* or *home* position, with fingers closed.

Note that the initial state is specified at the modeler level only. The initial state becomes the first snapshot at the emulator level, while the database is initially empty.

5.3.1.2. Emulating the Input Sequence

The operator sequence is given as a list of fully instantiated primitive operator schemata. In a real system, assuming the teach pendant implements the same command set as the ARMS primitive operator set, such an operator sequence may be read directly from the robot arm teach pendant. Thus the user interface of an ARMS implementation using a real robot arm would be identical to the user interface of robot teach-by-guiding systems currently in industrial use.[17]

The system reads in each element of the input sequence. As each operator is read in, it is passed on to the emulator level. The emulator constructs a new snapshot of the latest workspace that reflects the new state of the ARMS world after executing the input primitive. Each snapshot at the emulator level is a storage-efficient copy of the workspace at the modeler level. No changes are made at the schema level.

5.3.1.3. Building the Causal Model

The understander can best be described as a bottom-up inferential process that describes, using higher level operators, the context in which the lower level input operators are occurring. In this sense, it is very similar to those natural-language story-understanding systems which attempt to describe the context of an input story [51-54]. The understander operates entirely at the schema level; all interaction with the emulator and modeler levels is handled through the database.

The selection of a context with which to account for the input sequence has the potential for combinatorial explosion. This problem is usually termed the *frame-* or *schema-selection problem* [42]. What is needed is a method that restricts the amount of work done, a way to guide the selection process. Such methods are called *schema-activation methods.* While various methods have been proposed by natural-language researchers [38, 52, 54, 55], there are some key quirks of the robotics domain that can be used to advantage in devising an activation strategy.

5.3.1.3.1. Predictive Understanding

For the most part, natural-language story-understanding takes place in a *predictive* framework. This is necessary, since the inputs to a story system are rift with gaps that must be filled by inference chains. For example, consider the input

John bought a gun;
John forced Mary into the car;

---

[17] Any sequence produced in this manner would probably contain many extra input primitives. These noisy inputs would arise naturally from the expert's successive approximation of the proper position. The ARMS system is insensitive to this kind of noise.

is probably best understood in context with a set of intervening states:

John bought a gun;
John loaded the gun with ammunition;
John pointed the gun at Mary;
Mary knew that John was pointing a gun at her;
John told Mary to get into the car;
Mary decided to get into the car to avoid being shot;

and so on. The understander must by necessity be to some degree predictive, or the intervening inference chain cannot be constructed.

5.3.1.3.2. Nonpredictive Understanding

Unlike natural-language understanding systems, learning-apprentice systems face a reduced version of the input-gap problem. The learning apprentice has access to every action taken by the external problem-solving agent: unless the operators are poorly understood, there are never any gaps in the input sequence. In addition, the learning apprentice need only worry about a single external problem-solving agent, thus removing any problems resulting from interactions between agents.

This learning apprentice is no exception: there are never any input gaps in the ARMS input sequence. Each step in the assembly sequence entered by the assembly expert on the teach pendant is echoed to the system. Hence, there is no need for the understander to be predictive.

Nonpredictive understanding means that schemata activate only after they are temporally completed in the observed input. This implies that the *activation conditions* for any higher level schema can be expressed in terms of whether the schema's goal was accomplished or not. This also implies that if any schema is checked for activation and its activation conditions are not met, it is not necessary to retain the schema for future checking: no schema is ever allowed to remain primed without being activated, and each primed schema is checked for activation only once.

5.3.1.3.3. The Schema-Activation Mechanism

The schema activation algorithm used by ARMS works as follows (see Figure 5.2):

(1) The next observed input is read and an instantiated version of the corresponding primitive operator schemata I_i is added to the causal model. The time value t is incremented by one tick. Each of the operator templates on its suggestion list is instantiated and pushed on the *suggested schema list*. Note that when instantiating templates, many of the bindings of the input operator schema may

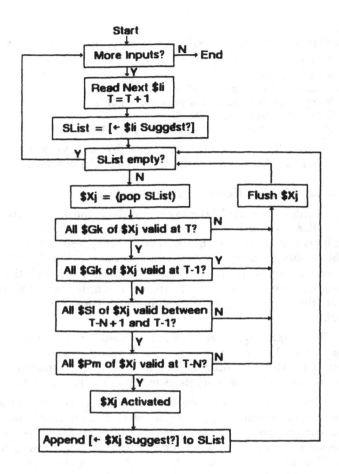

Activation Algorithm Flowchart

Figure 5.2

be transferred across the template equivalence list. Some bindings, however, may not yet be known and will have to be filled in later.

(2)   If the suggested schema list is empty and there are more inputs to be read, go back to Step 1. If there are no more inputs to be read, terminate. Otherwise, since the suggested schema list is not empty, continue with Step 3.

(3)   Pop the next operator schema $\$X_j$ off of the suggested schema list. Issue a request to the database for a state schema corresponding to

each goal Gk on the goal list of Xj. If there is some Gk that is not valid at time t, discard Xj and go to Step 2. Since the database always returns fully instantiated state schemata, make sure to transfer bindings from Gk back across the template equivalence list to Xj. In this fashion we gradually accumulate all the slots for Xj, which may have only been partially instantiated when suggested.

(4) Check each Gk for validity at time t-1. If every Gk is valid, discard Xj and go to Step 2.

(5) Starting at time t-1, unpack the subgoal poset of Xj backwards, issuing requests to the database for each subgoal Sl. Care must be taken to allow for legal permutations of subgoal ordering. Again, make sure to transfer bindings from each Sl back across the template equivalence list to Xj. If at some point some Sl cannot be validated, discard X and go to Step 2.

(6) Assuming the earliest subgoal Sl of Xj was valid at time $t-n+1$, issue requests for each precondition Pm to the database at time t-n. Transfer bindings from each Pm back across the template equivalence list to Xj. If there is some Pm which is not valid, discard Xj and go to Step 2.

(7) The instantiated composite operator schema Xj has now *activated* with a *scope* n time ticks. Instantiate all the operator schema templates on the suggestion list of Xj, being careful to carry any bindings from Xj across to the new suggestions. Append these new suggestions to the suggested schema list and go back to Step 2.

Note that the activation algorithm keeps on Xj the pointers to each instantiated Gk, Sl and Pm. This constitutes part of the causal model from which the explanation will be extracted. An example of a causal model is shown in Figure 5.3.

5.3.2. The Generalizer

The *generalizer* takes as its input the goal specification given by the expert and the causal model produced by the understander. If the episode meets the *learning criteria*, the generalizer will produce a new composite operator schema that can be used both in understanding and planning. In addition, in some cases a new physical joint schema will be produced as a side effect of the generalization process.

The procedure followed by the generalizer is outlined in Figure 5.4.

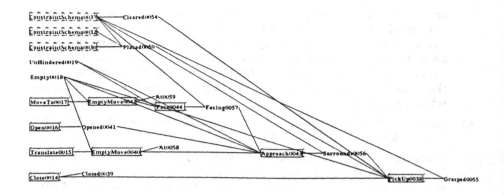

Portion of Causal Model

This figure represents a part of the causal model built (for a particular instance of $Pick-Up) using the non-predicitive ARMS schema activation algorithm. The unboxed nodes correspond to state schemata, the nodes in the dashed boxes are constraint schemata, and the boxed nodes correspond to operator schemata. The boxed nodes on the left edge of the figure represent the primitive operator schemata of the observed input sequence (with time increasing down the page).

Figure 5.3

5.3.2.1. The Verification Process

The first task the generalizer faces is to ascertain whether the observed episode really meets the goal specification given by the expert. This *verification process* entails applying the ARMS domain theory in order to justify how the goal specification is embodied in the physical structure assembled during the observed episode.

Recall the goal specification is given as an abstract schema joint template. This is easily transformed into an instantiated abstract joint schema which may, however, not have all of its slots filled. The abstract joint schema represents a mathematical characterization of the final assembly in terms of its degrees of freedom. The goal of the verification process is to find a valid physical joint schema instance which corresponds to the abstract joint schema instance partially specified by the expert.

There are four possible cases to consider:

(1) *Goal recognized during observation*: The instantiated abstract joint schema matches a physical joint schema instance already in the database. If this occurs, it indicates that a schema for

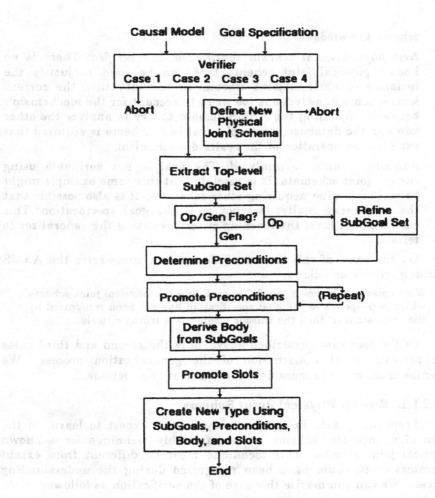

Generalization Flowchart

Figure 5.4

understanding how the goal was achieved already exists. This case does not meet the learning criteria, causing the generalizer to terminate.

(2) *Known physical joint schema verified*: The instantiated abstract joint schema is used to index a physical joint schema which can be successfully instantiated and validated. In this situation, the verification process completes successfully, using existing joint

schema knowledge.

(3)   *New physical joint schema constructed and verified*: There is no known physical joint schema that can be used to justify the instantiated abstract joint schema. In this situation, the current joint schema knowledge is too weak to account for the mechanism's behavior. By using the ARMS domain theory to analyze the other joints in the database, a new physical joint schema is acquired that explains the operation of the realized mechanism.

(4)   *Assembly cannot be analyzed*: The goal is not verifiable using current joint schemata. It is possible that this same example might be verifiable after acquiring other schemata. It is also possible that the mechanism really does not meet the goal specification. This case does not meet the learning criteria, causing the generalizer to terminate.

On the basis of this case analysis, we can summarize the ARMS learning criteria as follows:

If an episode achieves a verifiable goal, and the physical joint schema which corresponds to the goal specification has not been recognized by the understander, then the episode meets the learning criteria.

Of the four cases described above, only the second and third cases are relevant to this discussion of the generalization process. We describe these cases in more detail in the next two sections.

5.3.2.1.1. Known Physical Joint Schema

From an episode in this category we can expect to learn, in the form of an operator schema, a new assembly technique for a known physical joint schema. This technique must be different from extant operators or it would have been recognized during the understanding process. We can summarize this case of the verification as follows:

(1)   From the abstract joint schema instance index the collection of physical joint schemata which describe known ways to physically realize the desired mechanical behavior. For example, while the abstract joint schema $RigidJoint describes the mechanical behavior of a zero degree of freedom joint between two pieces, the physical joint schema $RigidJointA describes how this can be constructed by inserting one piece into the other.

(2)   Remove from this first set those instances which do not meet the constraints attached to the physical joint schemata. For the widget assembly, attached to $RigidJointA are constraints describing the relations that must hold between the two pieces of the joint. These are the constraints that ensure, for example, that the shaft radius

of the inserted piece must match the hole radius in the other piece.

(3)   Issue a request to the database for every remaining physical joint schema instance. The database attempts to validate each request, and, if successful, returns fully instantiated joint schemata.

As soon as a physical joint schema is validated, the verification process is complete, and no other validation requests are issued. Note that as a side effect of the validation process, the instantiated physical joint schema returned contains pointers to its substantiator set.

5.3.2.1.2. New Physical Joint Schema

If no known physical joint schema can be validated, the system attempts to explain how the mechanism works using domain knowledge about how joints and degrees of freedom combine. If successful, this step results in the addition to the schema library of a new physical joint schema indexed by the abstract joint schema used in the goal specification. This kind of learning is an example of *explanation-based specialization*. The verification process in this situation goes as follows:

(1)   From the physical joint schemata recognized during the observation phase, attempt to construct one or more *kinematic chains* relating the two pieces of the goal specification. A kinematic chain is a transitive relation on joint schemata.

(2)   Reduce the number of kinematic chains to one by removing those chains which contain physical joint schemata that subsume members of other chains. For example, if one chain contains joint Ji and another chain contains joints Jk and Jl which constitute the substantiator set of Ji, remove the chain containing Ji. In this fashion, the remaining chain will contain the lowest possible level of joint schema. If more than one such chain exists, terminate the verification process unsuccessfully.[18]

(3)   Collect all of the constituent degrees of freedom from the lone remaining kinematic chain.

(4)   Match this degree of freedom set with the expected degree of freedom set determined from the abstract joint schema corresponding to the goal specification. If no match can be found, terminate the verification process unsuccessfully.

(5)   Attempt to cancel each of the unmatched degrees of freedom from the kinematic chain by limiting their ranges. A degree of freedom

---

[18] Recall from Section 4.1.4 that the domain theory only accounts for open kinematic chains. Multiple chains at this point imply the presence of a closed kinematic chain.

ceases to be relevant as soon as its range of motion falls below a built-in tolerance. Reduction of the range can only take place if the degree of freedom previously contained a soft bound. By recalculating the soft bound, taking all of the pieces of the chain into account, interactions between chain elements may transform a soft bound into a hard bound with a limited range. If this step fails, terminate the verification process unsuccessfully.

(6)   Establish a new physical joint schema with members of the chain as substantiators. In addition, add constraints to the new joint schema that describe how degrees of freedom from the substantiators are canceled, or otherwise relate to the new physical joint schema.

As an example, consider the widget of Chapter 2. The goal specification is given as an instance of $RevoluteJoint, an abstract joint schema. As is the case in Chapter 2, assume that no known physical joint schema exists which properly characterizes this revolute joint. Thus, no verification is possible by following the procedure outlined in the previous section.

At the end of the understanding process, however, there are two recognized physical joint schema instances: an instance of $RigidJointA and an instance of $CylindricalJointA. These two joints form an open kinematic chain between $BoredBlock1 and $Washer1. A naive kinematic analysis of the degrees of freedom contained by the open kinematic chain shows that the revolute degree of freedom from $CylindricalJointA matches the required revolute degree of freedom for $RevoluteJoint. The prismatic degree of freedom from $CylindricalJointA is so constrained by $RigidJointA as to cease to be viable.

Given this kinematic analysis, we establish a new physical joint schema $RevoluteJointA that describes a method for implementing the joint behavior characterized by $RevoluteJoint. $RevoluteJointA in effect says that to make a $RevoluteJoint, make a $CylindricalJointA and restrict its degree of freedom using a $RigidJointA. $CylindricalJointA and $RigidJointA become the substantiator set for the new schema $RevoluteJointA.

The new schema is added to the schema library, and those constraints relating the pieces involved in the joint which were relevant to the kinematic analysis are included in the new schema. Note that while $RevoluteJoint relates two pieces (e.g., $BoredBlock1 and $Washer1), $RevoluteJointA relates an additional piece (e.g., $Peg1) to this piece set. Therefore $RevoluteJointA is applicable to any set of three pieces having the requisite interpiece constraints.

Note that if $RigidJointA and $CylindricalJointA could not be recognized during understanding, this analysis could not take place, and this episode would fall into the fourth verification category described above. In the ARMS system, the recognition of $RigidJointA and $CylindricalJointA depends on other acquired composite operator schemata. Therefore, at some later time (once the system has a chance to acquire these other operators), this episode would be ripe for learning.

We note two important points:

(1) The ARMS system is capable of using acquired schemata in understanding, and therefore in learning other, more complex, schemata.

(2) What cannot be understood now may well be understood later after the system has a chance to acquire more schemata. The ARMS system is very much characterized by learning one small step at a time, but without limiting the eventual extent of learned behavior.

5.3.2.2. Extracting the Explanation

As a result of the verification process, a valid physical joint schema is related to the abstract joint schema representing the goal specification. As part of the validation procedure, this physical joint schema contains a set of pointers to substantiators in the causal model. These substantiators constitute the *top-level subgoal set*.

We begin by ordering the top-level subgoal set on the basis of a causal dependency analysis. This causal analysis determines if there are any ordering dependencies between substantiator joints by examining the joint bounds. In the widget example described above, this analysis require that $CylindricalJointA occur before $RigidJointA, since $RigidJointA is used to impose constraints on a degree of freedom belonging to $CylindricalJointA.

To extract the explanation from the causal model, it is sufficient to follow the pointers established during the understanding process from the top-level subgoal set all the way back to the primitive operator inputs. The relevant pointers are those connecting operators to their subgoals and bodies, and connecting states to their achieving operators. Note that an explanation should also contain pointers to all of the constraint schemata supporting states in the explanation.

5.3.2.3. Building a New Operator Schema

Given the (ordered) top-level subgoal set, and therefore access to the explanation, a new composite operator schema is created so that this goal may be achieved and/or recognized in future episodes. This is an

example of *explanation-based generalization.*

The difficulty lies in determining exactly at what level of abstraction the new schema should be created. This question reflects the *generality/operationality tradeoff*, an important issue for explanation-based learning research. As with all tradeoffs, there appears to be no good single solution. It is likely that application-specific traits will determine the most opportune level of representation.

The ARMS system is capable of producing either a very general composite operator schema, or a more operational version of the composite operator schema. This aspect of the generalizer's behavior is governed by the *generality/operationality tradeoff flag* that can be set by the expert.

If the generality/operationality flag is set, ARMS produces the most general schema it can by using the top-level subgoal set as the explanation for this episode. No attempt is made to analyze the interdependencies present in the lower levels of this explanation.

If the flag is reset, the generalizer inserts an extra step at this point that expresses the new schema at a level where no shared substructures exist. In other words, beginning from the top-level subgoal set, descend the explanation structure to a level where no shared substructures exist between schemata at that level (see Figures 5.5 and 5.6). The state schemata at this level become the subgoal set of the new composite operator schema.

At the top level of the widget example, there are many shared substructures: consider, for example, the schema which represents grasping $Peg1. $Peg1 is manipulated in a manner that serves both $CylindricalJointA and $RigidJointA. Therefore, the grasping state is a shared substructure of the top-level subgoals. If we descend the explanation structure to the level of grasping $Peg1, there are no longer any shared substructures.

Note that this descent into the explanation which produces a new subgoal set is order-preserving: the new subgoal set will not violate the results of the causal dependency analysis performed at the joint schema level.

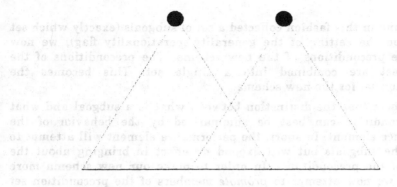

Level with Shared Substructures in Explanation

The two elements of the top-level subgoal set in this illustrative example are shown as black nodes. Their respective explanation substructures are outline as triangular subtrees. Shared substructure is represented by the overlapping sections of the subtrees. When producing the more general new schema, the generalizer uses the black nodes of the top-level subgoal set as the subgoal set model for the new schema.

Figure 5.5

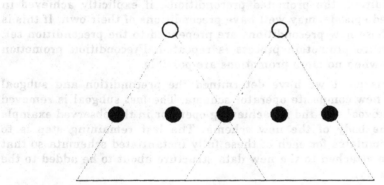

Level with No Shared Substructures in Explanation

The two elements of the top-level subgoal set are represented as white nodes at the root position of two overlapping explanation subtrees. When producing the more operational new schema, the generalizer descends into the explanation structure until it can produce a subgoal set (represented here as black nodes) with no shared substructure. This set then becomes the subgoal set model for the new schema.

Figure 5.6

Having in this fashion collected a set of subgoals (exactly which set depends on the setting of the generality/operationality flag), we now collect the preconditions of the new schema. The preconditions of the subgoal set are combined into a single set. This becomes the precondition set for the new schema.

We note that the distinction between what is a subgoal and what is a precondition can best be summarized by the behavior of the performance element. In short, the performance element will attempt to achieve the subgoals but will expend no effort in bringing about the validity of the preconditions. In order to make our new schema more powerful, we now attempt to *promote* members of the precondition set into subgoals according to the following *precondition promotion criteria*:

> If a precondition was achieved in the observed episode, it is prepended to the ordered list of subgoals. In addition, if a precondition was fortuitously true at the beginning of the observed episode, but a plan exists for achieving it, then it is also prepended to the subgoal set.

Note that prepending preconditions to the subgoal set is order-preserving.

In addition, the promoted preconditions, if explicitly achieved in the observed episode, may well have preconditions of their own. If this is the case, these new preconditions are prepended to the precondition set, and the entire promotion process is repeated. Precondition promotion terminates when no more promotions are possible.

At this point we have determined the precondition and subgoal sets of the new composite operator schema. The last subgoal is removed from the subgoal set, and its achieving operator in the observed example becomes the body of the new schema. The last remaining step is to generate templates for each of these fully instantiated schemata so that they can be attached to the new data structure about to be added to the schema library.

The generation of schema templates raises one more issue: the augmentation of the slot set in the physical joint schema for the new operator schema. We term this process the *slot promotion process*. The ARMS system creates a slot in the new operator schema for every slot in the physical joint schema it achieves. In addition, if any precondition or subgoal filler matches a filler in another precondition or subgoal, a slot is added to the new operator schema to carry this equivalence.

5.3.2.4. Meeting the Retention Criteria

At this point, the generalizer is ready to add the newly created schema to the schema library. The retention criteria evaluate whether a newly acquired schema is worth keeping or not. For the ARMS system, the retention criterion is always met: e.g., if the generalizer gets this far, the new schema is always worth keeping.

5.3.2.5. Integrating Newly Acquired Schemata

The new composite operator schema must be added to the schema library in such a way that it can be used both in understanding and in planning. If integrated properly, the system should not be able to tell the difference from a built-in operator schema and a newly acquired operator schema.

To be useful in understanding, the new operator schema must be the object of some existing schema's suggestion pointer. A suggestion pointer, in the form of a schema template, is therefore created on the achieving operator for the last element in the top-level subgoal set. For the general case of the generality/operationality tradeoff flag, this corresponds to the body of the new composite operator schema. In the more operational case, the suggestion pointer resides on an operator schema that is not explicitly mentioned in the new composite operator schema.

To be useful in planning, the new operator schema must be the object of some existing state schema's plan pointer. The ARMS knowledge representation strategy dictates that the goal of any operator contain a plan pointer to that operator. A template is created to reference the new schema from its goal (a physical joint schema) and added to the goal's plan list. Note that the physical joint schema may have been pre-existent, or may also have just been added to the schema library during the verification process.

5.3.2.6. Meeting the Replacement Criteria

If the generalizer keeps adding new schemata to the schema library, the cost of the schema-activation mechanism will continue to grow monotonically. The replacement criteria govern the replacement of existing schemata with new schemata in the schema library. By using replacement criteria to manage the growth of the schema library, it should be possible to keep the schema-activation complexity within reasonable bounds. The ARMS system does not, however, implement any replacement criteria.

Chapter 6
The Arms Implementation

We now describe the implementation of the ARMS system. Unlike Chapters 4 and 5, the organization of this chapter does not follow the functional divisions implicit in the ARMS architecture. Here our description follows the divisions implicit in the ARMS implementation. This chapter is in essence a guidebook to the implementation of the system, and is intended serve as an aid in any eventual reconstruction effort. As one might expect in an object-oriented implementation, the functional units of Chapters 4 and 5 are distributed throughout the system: for this reason the casual reader is encouraged to skip directly to Chapter 7.

We begin with a brief word about the implementation language and a description of two special tools used throughout the system. Next, we discuss the world modeler implementation, the graphics subsystem implementation, and the implementation of the schema system. Finally, we describe top-level access to the ARMS implementation.

6.1. A Note About the Implementation Language

The ARMS system runs on a Xerox 1109 DandeTiger lisp machine. It is implemented using LOOPS [56], an object-oriented programming language embedded in INTERLISP-D [57]. LOOPS provides object-oriented, rule-oriented, and access-oriented extensions to INTERLISP-D. The choice of implementation languages is not tremendously relevant, since, in addition to LISP, only the object-oriented aspect of LOOPS was used extensively in the development of the system.

For the purpose of our discussion, we avoid explicit references to LOOPS or INTERLISP-D. Instead, we define a generic terminology and syntax which describe only that subset of the language that is necessary for implementing the system.[19]

Our implementation language is basically a *frame language* [58-62]. It consists of a set of *frames* arranged in a *semantic hierarchy*. The structure and behavior of a particular frame depend on the position it occupies in the hierarchy. The hierarchy affects a frame by means of the *inheritance* mechanism.

The ARMS program consists of a set of frames, called *types*, arranged in the hierarchy. Each type is an abstract definition of a collection of similar frames. A type is always denoted with a "$" followed by a type name (e.g., $Type). Each type has a list of *super types* (or simply *supers*) that describe the position of the type in the hierarchy.

The types serve as templates for the creation of *tokens*. Each token represents a particular, unique object. A token is always denoted with a "$" followed by a name and a numeric identifier. The name is often, but not always, the same name as the token's type: thus, $Type1 denotes a token of type $Type. There are, however, cases where a more mnemonic name is used. For example, $Peg1, $Washer1, $Block1 and $BoredBlock1 all denote tokens of type $Piece.

A token always belongs to one and only one type. The structure and behavior of a token are determined by its type, and, through inheritance, by the supers of its type. Not all types, however, can be instantiated as tokens. Certain types, called *abstract types*, serve only as place holders in the inheritance hierarchy. Abstract types permit tokens of their subtypes to inherit their structure and/or behavior.

Each type may define *token slots*, *type slots*, and/or *procedures*. These features are inherited by tokens belonging to this type or its subtypes. Inheritance is resolved by tracing a token's ancestry upwards through the inheritance hierarchy described by the supers of its type. The preference order for inheritance is left-to-right along the supers list to the lowest shared type (see Figure 6.1).

A *token slot*, usually simply termed a *slot*, contains a pointer. Every token of this particular type, or any subtype of this type, has access to a copy of this slot. We will denote a token slot by prefacing its name with a ":" (e.g., :TokenSlot). A token slot may have some default initial value associated with it.

A *type slot* also contains a pointer. Every token of this particular type, or any subtype of this type, shares access to this same slot. A type slot is denoted by prefacing its name with "::" (e.g., ::TypeSlot). A type

---

[19] The reader familiar with LOOPS will notice many similarities between our syntax and that of LOOPS.

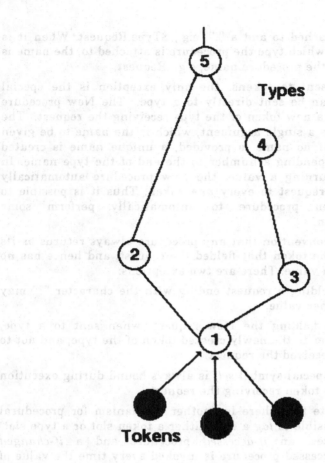

Inheritance Order

Figure 6.1

slot also has some initial value, although the notion of default is less significant here than in the token slot case.

A *procedure*, written in LISP, can also be attached to a type. This *procedural attachment* defines how a particular token behaves upon receipt of a *request*. The association between a request and the procedure it invokes is made when attaching the procedure to the type. Like for slots, a particular token's response to a given request is determined by the inheritance hierarchy. We denote a procedure name, which is always the same as the request that invokes it, by prefacing it with the type is attached to and a ".", e.g., $Type.Request. When it is clear by the context which type the procedure is attached to, the name is shortened to simply the procedure name, e.g., Request.

Requests are sent to tokens: the only exception is the special request New that can be sent directly to a type. The New procedure returns as its value a new token of the type receiving the request. The New procedure takes a single argument, which is the name to be given to the new token. If no name is provided, a unique name is created automatically by appending a number to the end of the type name. In addition, before returning a value, the New procedure automatically sends a NewToken request to every new token. Thus it is possible to write a NewToken procedure to automatically perform some initialization function.

We adopt the convention that any procedure always returns as its value a pointer to the token that fielded the request, and hence has no intrinsic information value. There are two exceptions:

(1)   A procedure fielding a request ending with the character "?" may return some other value.

(2)   The procedure fielding the New request, when sent to a type, returns a pointer to the newly created token of the type, and not to the type that received the request.

Note that the special symbol *self* is always bound during execution of a procedure to the token receiving the request.

Finally, we note that there is another mechanism for procedural attachment: it is possible to *tag* a slot (either a token slot or a type slot) with two procedures: an *if-accessed* procedure and a *if-changed* procedure. The if-accessed procedure is invoked every time the value of the slot is read, while the if-changed procedure is invoked when the value of the slot is written.

The reader will have no doubt noticed the similarity in the language terminology defined above and common schema terminology (see Appendix B). Fortunately, the terms are often interchangeable since, as we will see in the section describing schema implementation, the implementation of a schema slot is, in fact, a token slot.

6.2. Optimization Tools

There are two extremely important mechanisms, implemented as types, that are used to increase the performance of the ARMS system. Normally, one would discuss these programming tricks as a footnote to a straightforward description of a naive version of the system. However, since this chapter is aimed at facilitating reconstruction efforts, and since the use of these tools pervades the rest of the implementation, we choose to discuss them first.

The first tool, $MatchMixin (see Table 6.1), is used by the schema database mechanism (described in Sections 5.1.2. and 6.6.3.) in order to match different instances of state schemata. The ability to determine when two schemata refer to the same thing is important when implementing the database mechanism's schema cache.

The second tool, $LazyCopy (see Table 6.2), is used by the history mechanism (described in Sections 4.2.3. and 6.6.3.) in order to maintain layered copies of the solid modeler.

Both of these tools key on the classic space vs. time programming tradeoff; note, however, that they sit on the opposite sides of the issue. The state schema database cache saves time in a computationally-intensive process by caching data structures, and, therefore, increasing storage requirements. The history mechanism saves space in a storage-intensive process by compressing the data structures, with concomitant increase in access time.

6.2.1. $MatchMixin

The matching mechanism permits comparison of two tokens, returning self if the two tokens represent the same thing. In order to match, two tokens must be of the same type, and a selected subset of their slots must match recursively.

The matcher is implemented as an abstract type called $MatchMixin. $MatchMixin is used as one of a set of supers for other types. By placing a type beneath $MatchMixin in the inheritance hierarchy, we endow tokens of the new type with the ability to be matched against other tokens. The matching mechanism relies on a type slot ::MatchSlots that indicates which slots in the token are significant for the matcher.

$MatchMixin has a single procedure, Matches?, that takes two arguments: the first being another token and the second being a schema

Table 6.1 $MatchMixin		
TypeSlots	::MatchSlots	
Procedures	Matches?	returns self or NIL

template. If only the first argument is given, then self is returned when it matches the first argument directly. If a second argument is given, then Matches? returns self if a new token created from the second argument (a template) using the first argument as requester would match self.

In the absence of a second argument, the Matches? procedure first compares the type of each token. If the types are identical, then Matches? recursively compares fillers for each slot on ::MatchSlots from self with the corresponding fillers from the first argument. If all of these also match, then Matches? returns self; otherwise, it returns NIL.

If a second argument is present, then the header of the second argument is compared against the type of self. If these are the same, then Matches? recursively compares, for every slot on ::MatchSlots, the filler from self with the corresponding filler from the first argument as given in the binding equivalences of the second argument. As before, Matches? returns either self or NIL.

Note that this second case could be handled naively by simply creating a new token from the first and second arguments and then resorting to the first procedure. This would result in many extra tokens being generated and subsequently discarded. As implemented, this procedure will never create a new token and, therefore, saves storage.

Since some of the slot fillers are nontokens (e.g., they may be lists of tokens, atoms, numbers, etc.), special care must be taken with the recursive matching step. The recursive step is implemented with a separate function Match, that takes two arguments and returns the first if it matches the second. Implementation of the Match function is straightforward, the only possible difficulty being insuring that lists match any permutation of themselves.

6.2.2. $LazyCopy

The lazy copy mechanism permits storage-efficient copying of tokens belonging to types below $LazyCopy in the inheritance hierarchy. The general idea is to produce a new token, of type $LazyCopy, that behaves just like the original token except for certain preselected token slots. Those token slots are duplicated, so that the new copy may have a different value than the original. Any reference to an unduplicated slot is referred back to the original token, while any reference to one of the duplicated slots is handled locally by the copy.

To make this process efficient, slot duplication is a lazy process, in the sense that duplication takes place only when that particular slot filler is accessed. In other words, when accessing a duplicated slot, if no filler is found locally, the filler is found in the original and duplicated at the copy at access time. Naturally, if one is writing a new filler at a copy no access to the original is needed: one simply creates the duplicate slot on the copy and assigns it the new filler.[20]

The process is permitted to continue, whereby a copy can be made of a copy and so forth. When a chain of copies is produced, only the very first token is not of type $LazyCopy; this is termed the *base instance*. Each successive copy is a token of type $LazyCopy.

There are four potential problems when implementing $LazyCopy:

(1) When referring to an unselected token slot in a copy belonging to a chain of copies, we should bypass all of the layers and go directly to the base instance. Note that this means access to selected slots may cascade through many layers before finding the most recent filler, while duplicating the slot/filler on each copy traversed.

(2) Procedural requests fielded by a token of type $LazyCopy must be handled by the procedure attached to the type of the base instance. The procedure must, however, be invoked in the context of the $LazyCopy's slot fillers, rather than those of the base instance.

(3) Coreferential pointers must remain coreferential. For example, if $A, $B, and $C are all subtypes of $LazyCopy and tokens $Ai and $Bj both refer to $Ck as a filler, any copies of $Ai and $Bj must refer to a unique copy of $Ck.

<table>
<tr><td colspan="3" align="center">**Table 6.2**
$LazyCopy</td></tr>
<tr><td>*Supers*</td><td>$MatchMixin</td><td></td></tr>
<tr><td>*TypeSlots*</td><td>::LazySlots
::MatchSlots</td><td>used by copy process
only :Base used for matching</td></tr>
<tr><td>*Slots*</td><td>:Base
:CopyOf
:CopyMap</td><td>points to base token
points to copied token
points to token equivalence mappings
   for this generation</td></tr>
<tr><td>*Procedures*</td><td>Copy
Match?</td><td>make next generation copy of self
for matching mechanism</td></tr>
</table>

---

[20] Subsequent releases of the LOOPS language define a class $VirtualCopy that is very similar to our $LazyCopy type. The only difference appears to be in the lazy duplication: $VirtualCopy creates the duplicate slots at copy time.

(4)   Behavior of a $LazyCopy token under the match operation described in Section 6.2.1 must be reasonable.

We handle the first two problems in the same fashion: any access to a token of type $LazyCopy, whether for filler information or procedure execution, is intercepted at the $LazyCopy and forwarded, along with the local slot fillers, to the base instance.

In order to address the third problem, the procedure for creating a lazy copy must insure that, for each generation, there is a single unique token for every token of the previous generation. The mechanism that enforces this uniqueness consists of a :CopyMap slot that points to a mapping of tokens from the previous generation to their counterparts in this generation. This mapping is an association list that is shared by every token in a particular generation: it is maintained using LISP destructive list operations, such that additions to the mapping are immediately accessible to all tokens in a given generation.

The fourth issue is easily dealt with: in order to match a lazy copy against a token it is sufficient to make $LazyCopy a subtype of $MatchMixin and to force its ::MatchSlots type slot to contain only :Base. There are then two different cases to consider:

(1)   If two tokens are both of type $LazyCopy, then they must have the same :Base filler for a match.

(2)   If only one of the tokens is of type $LazyCopy then the other token must be the same as the filler of the $LazyCopy token's :Base slot.

This is implemented as a Matches? procedure attached to $LazyCopy. By placing $LazyCopy below $MatchMixin in the hierarchy, we insure that this procedure is invoked (rather than $MatchMixin.Matches?) if a token of type $LazyCopy fields the Matches? request. In addition, a small change is made to $MatchMixin.Matches so that Matches? requests with a token of type $LazyCopy as the second argument are forwarded to this new procedure with their arguments reversed.

6.3. Implementing the Solid Modeler

The modeler consists of code for the representation and manipulation of objects in three-space, implemented over several different types. The semantic hierarchy for this part of the ARMS system is shown in Figure 6.2.

Before discussing the modeler, we take a moment to review the homogeneous coordinate system used to represent points in three space in order to establish some basic terms.

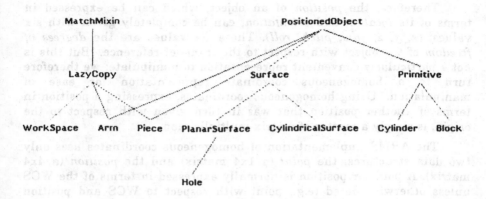

Solid Modeler Semantic Hierarchy

Figure 6.2

6.3.1. Homogeneous Coordinates

The ARMS system uses *homogeneous coordinates* to represent points in three-space. The homogeneous coordinate system represents a problem in *n*-space as a problem in $(n+1)$-space. Manipulations of the problem are all done in $(n+1)$-space, and the solution is projected back into *n*-space. Our discussion of this technique is limited to a short intuitive description. For a thorough review of the mathematics involved, see [63].

Assume that there is some base right-handed Cartesian coordinate system from which everything is measured. Call this origin the *world coordinate system* (or *WCS*). Now assume you are trying to describe the position of an object with respect to the WCS. We represent the object being positioned by its own right-handed coordinate system.

We can now describe the location of the object using a triple of values *(x, y, z)* to indicate the location of the origin of the object coordinate system. But this does not tell us anything about the orientation of the coordinate system: is it lying on its side? Is it upside down? By establishing some reference state for the orientation of the object coordinate system (such as the orientation of the WCS), we can give angles of rotation about the three Cartesian axes, or *(yaw, pitch, roll)*, that describe the orientation of the coordinate system with respect to the reference state. Note that the order these rotations are applied in is significant: we choose to apply them always in left-to-right order about the X, Y, and Z axes, respectively.

Therefore, the *position* of an object, which can be expressed in terms of its *location* and *orientation*, can be completely given with six values: *(x, y, z, yaw, pitch, roll)*. These six values are the *degrees of freedom* of the object with respect to the frame of reference. But this is not a particularly convenient representation to manipulate: we therefore turn to a homogeneous coordinate representation for ease of manipulation. Using homogeneous coordinates, expressing a position in terms of another position that was in turn given with respect to the origin, is simply a matter of matrix multiplication.

The ARMS implementation of homogeneous coordinates uses only two data structures: the *point* (a 1x4 matrix) and the *position* (a 4x4 matrix). A point or position is normally expressed in terms of the WCS unless otherwise noted (e.g., point with respect to WCS and position with respect to WCS become simply point and position, respectively). To represent a vector, ARMS uses a point data structure to represent the tip of the vector in some frame of reference.

Functions are provided to create points and positions, access and change their individual elements, and calculate dot products, Cartesian distance and vector distance between pairs of points and/or positions. Positions can be inverted, translated to the origin, and they may also have their normals (a unit vector along the Z axis) extracted. Finally, vectors (which are indistinguishable from points in structure) may be normalized, e.g., rescaled into unit length vectors.

In addition, a set of comparison functions on two positions is provided. These functions use a global tolerance value to avoid problems with computer arithmetic roundoff error. The comparison functions provided can be used to test whether

(1)   the two positions are *equal*;

(2)   the Z axes of the two positions are *colinear*;

(3)   the Z axes of the two positions are *parallel*;

(4)   the Z axes of the two positions are *orthogonal*;

(5)   the two positions are colinear and their x axes are parallel (*aligned*);

(6)   or the XY planes of the two positions are *coplanar*.

6.3.2. $WorkSpace

A token of type $WorkSpace (see Table 6.3) represents a snapshot of the ARMS world at a given time. We define the *world coordinate system* *(WCS)* as the coordinate frame of reference of the workspace surface. This is the origin with respect to which all other points in the world are defined.

The slots on $WorkSpace correspond directly with the physical components of the ARMS robot world discussed in Section 4.1.1.2.:

(1)   The :Contents slot contains a list of the pieces in the workspace, where each piece is represented by a token of type $Piece.

(2)   The :Arm slot points to a token of type $Arm which represents the robot arm.

(3)   The :Surface slot points to a token of type $PlanarSurface which represents the table top.

(4)   The :View slot points to a token of type $View that manages the graphic display of the workspace. If :View is NIL, no graphic display is supported.

The procedures attached to the $WorkSpace type manipulate the world representation:

(1)   The AddPiece procedure adds a piece to the contents of the workspace, establishes support for the piece, and updates the graphics system if there is one. Note that AddPiece also tags the piece's :Position slot with an if-changed procedure if and only if there is a graphics system associated with this workspace. The if-changed procedure updates the picture of the piece on the screen whenever its position is changed.

(2)   The DeletePiece procedure is used to remove a piece from the workspace, again causing the appropriate changes to occur in an

Table 6.3 $WorkSpace		
Supers	$LazyCopy	
TypeSlots	::LazySlots	:Contents, :Arm, :View
Slots	:Contents :Surface :Arm :View	list of $Piece tokens $PlanarSurface token $Arm token pointer to graphic display
Procedures	AddPiece DeletePiece Input NewToken	add token to :Contents remove token from :Contents emulator: forwards command to :Arm initialization procedure

associated view.

(3)   The Input procedure is used by the ARMS emulator. It takes a primitive arm command as its argument and forwards the command to the filler of the :Arm slot (a token of type $Arm). The arm emulates the command, causing some changes to occur in self to reflect the changes wrought by the arm command.

(4)   The NewToken procedure is an initialization procedure invoked automatically when a new token of type $WorkSpace is created. It creates a new token of type $PlanarSurface and places this token on the :Surface slot. It also initializes the graphic system if there is to be a view for this workspace.

$WorkSpace is a subtype of $LazyCopy, supporting storage-efficient copies of a snapshot via the lazy copy mechanism described in Section 6.2.2. Since the position of pieces as well as the arm may change with time, the ::LazySlots type slot lists both :Contents and :Arm are marked as lazy slots for the lazy copy mechanism. Since the workspace surface is never changed or moved, it need not be included on ::LazySlots. The :View slot is included, since each world snapshot implies a different view of the workspace.

6.3.3. $PositionedObject

$PositionedObject (see Table 6.4) is the simplest type in the entire ARMS system. It contains the lone slot :Position that gives the position of any subtoken in terms of some coordinate frame of reference (usually the WCS). $PositionedObject is an abstract type; thus, no explicit tokens of this type are ever instantiated.

6.3.4. $Piece

Tokens of type $Piece (see Table 6.5) are used to represent the pieces manipulated by the robot arm. $Peg1, $Washer1, $BoredBlock1 and all the others mentioned in Chapter 2 are tokens of type $Piece. $Piece is a subtype of $PositionedObject, and therefore inherits a :Position slot. The :Position filler indicates where the piece represented

		Table 6.4 **$PositionedObject**
Slots	:Position	matrix representing 3D position

by this token is located with respect to the WCS.

The slots on $Piece describe the physical structure of the piece represented by a given token:

Table 6.5
$Piece

Supers	$PositionedObject $LazyCopy	
TypeSlots	::LazySlots	:Support, :SupportingSurface, :Position, :Segment
Slots	:Primitives	list of $Primitive tokens that define self
	:Surfaces	list of $Surface tokens belonging to self
	:Holes	list of $Hole tokens belonging to self
	:Support	$Piece token or $WorkSpace token on which self rests
	:SupportSurface	member of :Surfaces in contact with :Support
	:Mass	mass calculated from :Primitives
	:CenterOfMass	point wrt :Position
	:DisplayOps	3D wireframe specification
	:Segment	pointer to 2D projection of wireframe
Procedures	NewToken	computes :Surfaces, :Holes, :Mass, :CenterOfMass
	Support?	computes :Support, :SupportSurface
	Inside?	T if given point is inside self at current position
	Intersect?	T if given line intersects self at current position
	On?	T if given point is on self at current position
	Render	projects self on view
	GraspPosition?	planner: returns consistent grasping strategy for self
	Collisions?	used to find interpiece collisions

(1)   The :Primitives slot contains a list of tokens describing the CSG primitives which define this piece. The :Position slots on these tokens represent the position of the primitives with respect to the position of the piece.

(2)   The :Surfaces slot contains a list of tokens describing the surfaces (BRep) of the piece derived from the CSG primitives used to define the piece. The :Position slots of these tokens represent the positions of the surfaces with respect to the position of the piece.

(3)   The :Holes slot contains a list of tokens describing the holes in piece resulting from the application of the contained difference CSG operator to the piece's constituent primitives. The :Position slots of these tokens represent the positions of the holes with respect to the position of the piece.

(4)   The :Support slot points to either another token of type $Piece representing the piece underneath the current piece, or to the token of type $PlanarSurface representing the table top of the current workspace. This slot indicates what is providing the current piece with support.

(5)   The :SupportSurface slot points to the member of :Surfaces in contact with the :Support filler.

(6)   The :Mass slot contains the mass of the piece as computed from the mass of its constituent primitives.

(7)   The :CenterOfMass slot contains a matrix describing the center of mass with respect to the piece's frame of reference. This point is computed from the masses of the constituent primitives of the piece and is used to determine what is supporting the piece.

(8)   The :DisplayOps slot contains a list of 3D graphics commands which represent the wireframe outline of the piece. This is computed from the wireframes of the constituent primitives.

(9)   The :Segment slot contains a pointer to a token of type $Segment used by the graphics package to represent the 2D rendering of the 3D graphics commands in :DisplayOps.

The procedures attached to $Piece are used predominantly to support geometric operations on the piece.

(1)   The NewToken procedure is invoked when a new piece is created. It is this procedure that calculates the surfaces, holes, mass, and center of mass of a piece from its constituent primitives. Calculation of mass and center of mass are straightforward: recall that primitives which are removed using the CSG contained difference operator have a different effect on the center of mass

than those primitives added using the CSG disjoint union operator. The collection of surfaces and holes works as follows:

For each primitive in :Primitives:
Collect their Surfaces on surfaceList.
For every surface in surfaceList:
If surface's primitive is *solid*:
If surface is *covered* by another surface
on different solid primitive of :Primitives:
then discard it,
else retain it on self's :Surfaces.
Else if surface's primitive is not *solid*:
If surface is *covered* by another surface
on a different solid primitive of :Primitives:
then change surface into a hole and add to self's :Holes,
else invert its normal and retain it on self's :Surfaces.

There are procedures attached to the various surface types that are used to determine if one surface covers another surface.

NewToken is also responsible for initializing the graphics package. The :DisplayOps slot contains a set of 3D display operations which result in a wireframe representation of the piece. The :Segment slot points to a token of type $Segment (see Section 6.4.2).

(2) The Render procedure is used to project the 3D wireframe in the :DisplayOps into a 2D representation stored in the $Segment token, taking into account the current position of the piece and all of the viewing parameters of the current view (see Section 6.4.1). The interface to the graphics package is provided via the use of an if-changed procedure tagged onto the :Position slot of each token of type $Piece. When the piece is moved, its :Position slot value changes, and the if-changed procedure forces updating of the view. The :Position slot for a given $Piece token is tagged by the $WorkSpace.AddPiece procedure.

(3) The Support? procedure returns the support and supporting surface for self in a given workspace. This procedure, although extremely naive, is a compromise that works rather well due to the restricted nature of the piece tokens allowed by the modeler. The algorithm works as follows (see Figure 6.3):

Drop a line down from the :CenterOfMass wrt WCS.
Find the most distant intersection of this plumb line with self.
Identify the surface of this intersection as the :SupportSurface.
If there is contact between the :SupportSurface and workspace:
    then :Support is the workspace surface.
Else if there is contact between :SupportSurface and another piece:
    then :Support is the other piece.
    else :Support is NIL.

There are procedures attached to the various surface types which are used to calculate line/surface intersections as well as point/surface contact.

(4)   The Inside?, Intersect? and On? procedures are used to compute various geometric operations on the piece involving points and line segments. In general, they forward the same request onto the constituent parts of the piece, whether the relevant parts are surfaces, holes, or primitives.

(5)   The GraspPosition? procedure is used by the planner to return a legal grasping position for the piece at its current location. It takes many arguments, including a list of surfaces and primitives which must not be in contact with the gripper fingers or occluded by the

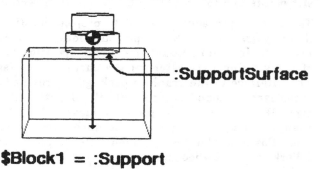

$Block1 = :Support

Illustration of $Piece Support? Algorithm

Figure 6.3

gripper palm. The GraspPosition? procedure returns an arm position which will allow the gripper to grasp the piece by opposing surfaces on one of self's primitives, without violating the requested free surface and primitive criteria.

(6) The Collisions? procedure is used to find collisions between self and other pieces in the workspace when self is projected along a given axis. This is used in finding bounds on the joints during the goal verification process.

The type $Piece is a subtype of $LazyCopy. Since the position of a piece changes with time, :Position is one of the ::LazySlots for tokens of type $Piece. Other lazy slots include :Support and :SupportSurface, which also change with time, and :Segment. By making :Segment a lazy slot, we retain the ability to display a view of the workspace at any time tick without further computation.

6.3.5. $Primitive

Tokens of types $Block and $Cylinder appear on the :Primitives slot of tokens of type $Piece. They are the basic building blocks of the CSG modeler. $Block and $Cylinder are subtypes of the abstract type $Primitive (see Table 6.6). They inherit :Piece, :Density, and :Solid? slots from $Primitive, and a :Position slot from $PositionedObject.

The value of :Position represents the position of the primitive with respect to the piece frame of reference (represented by the :Position slot attached to the piece). It is easy to calculate the position of a particular primitive by multiplying the position of the primitive by the position of the piece. Note that the value of this :Position slot, unlike the :Position slot of a token of type $Piece, never changes once the piece is defined!

Table 6.6 $Primitive		
Supers	$PositionedObject	
Slots	:Piece	$Piece token to which self belongs
	:Solid?	indicates CSG combination operator
	:Density	used to compute mass
Procedures	GenerateHolesAndSurfaces	initializes piece :Surfaces

Hence :Position is not a lazy slot when it belongs to tokens of subtypes of type $Primitive.[21]

The :Piece slot contains a pointer to the token of type $Piece to which this $Primitive token belongs. The :Solid? slot is T for solid CSG primitives, and NIL for nonsolid CSG primitives. The :Density slot is used in the calculation of mass for a given piece: each primitive is allowed to have a different value for its density, thereby changing the stability requirements for the piece.

6.3.6. $Block, $Cylinder

The $Block and $Cylinder types (see Tables 6.7 and 6.8) are very similar: the procedures attached to them have the same protocols and calling procedures, but differ internally due to the differing structure of the types themselves.

$Block contains :Width, :Height, and :Length slots, while $Cylinder contains :Radius and :Height slots. These slots taken together give the dimensions of the particular instance of the primitive. From these, values for the :Center and :Volume slots are computed. :Center gives the Cartesian position of the center of mass of this primitive (with respect to the position of the primitive), and is used in computing the

Table 6.7 $Block		
Supers	$Primitive	
Slots	:Width	X dimension
	:Length	Y dimension
	:Height	Z dimension
Procedures	Surfaces?	returns list of surfaces
	DisplayOps?	generates wireframe specification
	Insertable?	is self insertable in argument?
	Inserted?	is self inserted in other primitive?
	Aligned?	is self aligned with other primitive?
	Inside?	is position inside self?

---

[21] In fact, $Primitive does not contain $LazyCopy on its supers list. No slots belonging to $Primitive or any of its subtypes ever change once the piece has been defined.

	Table 6.8 $Cylinder	
Supers	$Primitive	
Slots	:Radius :Height	XY dimension Z dimension
Procedures	Surfaces? DisplayOps? Insertable? Inserted? Aligned? Inside?	returns list of surfaces generates wireframe specification is self insertable in argument? is self inserted in other primitive? is self aligned with other primitive? is position inside self?

center of mass of the piece. Both of these slots contain examples of tagged procedural attachment: their values are computed from the dimension slots using an if-accessed procedure.

The Surfaces? procedure returns a list of new $Surface tokens representing the surfaces for the given $Primitive token. Note that the $Surface tokens are created in such a manner as to reflect the dimensions of the primitive, and whether or not the primitive is solid. This procedure is invoked by $Piece.NewToken, and is only used at piece creation time.

The Inside? procedure takes a point and returns T if that point is inside the primitive, else it returns NIL. The Inserted? procedure is similar, except it compares the primitive with another primitive of the same type and returns T if one encloses the other: the enclosing primitive must not, of course, be solid. The Aligned? procedure compares the primitive with another primitive of the same type and returns T if the primitives are aligned on the same coordinate axes.

The Insertable? procedure compares self with another primitive or a hole and returns T unless there is no possible insertion of self in the argument. This is predominantly used as a test predicate for constraint schemata.

The DisplayOps? procedure is used to generate the proper 3D display operations which specify the wireframe of the primitive. The wireframe is computed using the dimensions of the given primitive. The DisplayOps? procedure is also invoked by $Piece.NewToken as part of the piece initialization process.

6.3.7. $Surface

The abstract type $Surface (see Table 6.9) exists in order to endow its subtypes, which represent the faces and holes of a piece, with :Piece, :Primitive, and :OpposingSurfaces slots. Note that these subtypes also inherit :Position slots, since $Surface is itself a subtype of $PositionedObject.

The :Piece and :Primitive slots point to the piece and primitive this surface token belongs to. Just as in the case of the $Primitive tokens, the :Position slot represents the position of the surface with respect to the position of the piece it belongs to. The :OpposingSurfaces slot contains a list of other tokens that represent other surfaces belonging to the same piece as self whose normals point in the opposing direction. This information is used by the $Piece.GraspPosition? procedure, and is initialized by the $Piece.NewToken procedure.

Given the restricted nature of the CSG primitives and combination operators, only two types of surfaces can ever arise in the ARMS solid modeler. These are represented by the types $PlanarSurface and $CylindricalSurface, which are subtypes of $Surface.

6.3.8. $PlanarSurface, $CylindricalSurface

Tokens of types $PlanarSurface and $CylindricalSurface (see Tables 6.10 and 6.11) appear on the :Surfaces slot of tokens of type $Piece. They represent the faces of the piece, and therefore constitute the BRep representation.

The :Type slot contains a keyword that indicates the type of planar surface (rectangular or round) or cylindrical surface (exterior or interior) that is represented by a given token. $Block primitives give rise to rectangular $PlanarSurface tokens, while $Cylinder primitives result in round $PlanarSurface and both types of $CylindricalSurface tokens. The dimensions of each token are determined by the $Piece.NewToken

<table>
<tr><td colspan="3" align="center">**Table 6.9**
$Surface</td></tr>
<tr><td>*Supers*</td><td>$PositionedObject</td><td></td></tr>
<tr><td>*Slots*</td><td>:Piece
:Primitive
:OpposingSurfaces</td><td>$Piece token to which self belongs
$Primitive token to which self belongs
list of opposing surfaces on same piece</td></tr>
</table>

Table 6.10
$PlanarSurface

Supers	$Surface	
Slots	:Type	one of Round or Rectangular
	:XDim	X dimension for Rectangular, radius for Round
	:YDim	Y dimension for Rectangular, null for Round
Procedures	CoLinear?	is self colinear with other surface?
	CoPlanar?	is self coplanar with other surface?
	Covers?	does self cover other surface?
	Intersect?	does line intersect self?
	On?	is point on self?
	Oppose?	does self oppose other surface?
	Overlap?	does self contact other surface?
	Parallel?	is self parallel with other surface?

Table 6.11
$CylindricalSurface

Supers	$Surface	
Slots	:Type	one of Exterior or Interior
	:Radius	radius of tubular surface
	:ZDim	height of tubular surface
Procedures	CoLinear?	is self colinear with other surface?
	CoPlanar?	is self coplanar with other surface?
	Covers?	does self cover other surface?
	Intersect?	does line intersect self?
	On?	is point on self?
	Oppose?	does self oppose other surface?
	Overlap?	does self contact other surface?
	Parallel?	is self parallel with other surface?

procedure in accordance with the dimensions of the primitives making up the piece.

The brunt of the geometric operations supported by the modeling system are implemented as procedures attached to these two types.

(1)   The CoLinear? procedure returns T if the given surface is colinear with self.

(2)   The CoPlanar? procedure returns T if the given surface is coplanar with self and has an opposing normal.

(3)   The Oppose? procedure is much like CoPlanar?, except any distance is allowed between the two parallel surfaces.

(4)   The Parallel? procedure returns T if the normal of the given surface is parallel with the normal of self.

(5)   The Covers? procedure returns T if the given surface is coplanar with self and its extent is covered by self.

(6)   The Overlap? procedure is much like Covers?, except the two surfaces must have opposing normals, and there need not be a covering: simple contact will suffice.

(7)   The Intersect? procedure returns the point where self intersects a given line segment, if any.

(8)   The On? procedure returns T if a given point is on self.

6.3.9. $Hole

Tokens of type $Hole (see Table 6.12) are used to represent openings in the pieces themselves: they result from the use of the CSG contained difference combination operator.

When a planar surface on a primitive that is the object of a contained difference operator is covered by another planar surface on the same piece, it is replaced with a token of type $Hole. The only holes allowed result from planar surfaces, and so, as one might expect, $Hole is a subtype of $PlanarSurface (thus permitting inheritance from that type). The only slot added by the $Hole type lists any other holes in the

Table 6.12 **$Hole**		
Supers	$PlanarSurface	
Slots	:OpposingHoles	exit hole, if any
Procedures	Swallows?	checks against surface

piece which resulted from the same contained difference operation and have an opposing normal: this implies that the primitive removed with the contained difference goes all the way through the piece.

The Swallows? procedure is the only procedure attached to $Hole. $Hole.Swallows? checks the hole against another surface and an axis, returning T only if the hole, when projected along the axis, covers the surface.

6.3.10. $Arm

A token of type $Arm (see Table 6.13) represents the idealized robot arm that manipulates the pieces in the workspace. It is a subtype of $PositionedObject, and therefore possesses a :Position slot that holds the current gripper position as measured at the hot spot.

The slots of $Arm are used to describe the size, shape, and configuration of the gripper.

(1)   The :Palm slot contains a token of type $Block representing the part of the gripper between the two fingers. The :Position slot of this token represents the position of the palm with respect to the gripper hot spot.

(2)   The :Fingers slot contains a list of two tokens of type $Block describing the two identical gripper fingers. The :Position slots of these tokens represent the positions of the fingers with respect to the hot spot.

(3)   The :Contacts slot contains a list of two points, given with respect to the hot spot, which are located on the tips of the two fingers. These contact points can be thought of as the two rubber pads found on the inner surfaces of the finger tips of many commercially available robot arm grippers.

(4)   The :Spread slot contains a number indicating the current aperture between the two fingers, as measured at the contact points.

(5)   The :MaxSpread slot contains a number giving the upper bound on the possible values of the :Spread slot.

(6)   The :FingerLength slot contains a number giving the maximum clearance between the palm and the finger tips.

(7)   The :PalmClearance slot contains a number giving the clearance between the palm of the gripper and any piece currently being held.

(8)   The :HeldPosition slot contains the position of any piece currently being held, given with respect to the gripper hot spot.

Table 6.13 $Arm		
Supers	$PositionedObject $LazyCopy	
TypeSlots	::LazySlots	:Contacts, :Spread, :PieceHeld, :HeldPosition, :Position, :WorkSpace, :Segment
Slots	:Palm	token of type $Block
	:Fingers	list of two tokens of type $Block
	:Contacts	list of two points wrt :Position at finger tips
	:Spread	current aperture between fingers
	:MaxSpread	maximum finger aperture
	:FingerLength	distance from hot spot to palm
	:PalmClearance	margin between palm and any piece held
	:PieceHeld	token of type $Piece being held by gripper, if any
	:HeldPosition	position wrt :Position of :PieceHeld
	:WorkSpace	token of type $WorkSpace containing self
	:Segment	for 3D graphics
	:DisplayOps	for 3D graphics
Procedures	Close	emulator: close fingers
	Open	emulator: open fingers
	MoveTo	emulator: change position
	Translate	emulator: change position along axis by delta
	Rotate	emulator: change position about axis by theta
	Render	projects self on view at position
	NewToken	initializes :Contacts, :Spread

(9)   The :WorkSpace slot contains a pointer to the workspace snapshot associated with this token.

(10) The :DisplayOps slot contains a list of 3D graphics commands which represent the wireframe outline of the gripper. This is computed from the wireframes of the constituent primitives. Note that unlike the :DisplayOps slot on a piece, the gripper's display

operations will change as the gripper changes finger configuration.

(11) The :Segment slot contains a pointer to a token of type $Segment used by the graphics package to represent the 2D rendering of the 3D graphics commands in :DisplayOps.

With a single exception, the procedures attached to $Arm are all used to implement the emulator. The emulator takes a primitive arm command and a workspace snapshot (usually a token of type $LazyCopy) and updates the workspace to reflect the effects of the execution of the primitive arm command input. Most of the changes made are to the slots on the $Arm token corresponding to the workspace, although some changes may result from modeling arm/piece interactions.

The emulator forwards a request corresponding to the arm input command to the :Arm filler from its workspace snapshot. Each arm primitive has a corresponding procedure attached to $Arm that modifies the workspace snapshot (and thus also the related arm) accordingly.

(1) The Close procedure closes the gripper fingers as far as possible within the current workspace snapshot given by :WorkSpace. Close may affect the fillers of the :Contacts and :Spread slots directly. In addition, Close will usually change the :Position slots of the tokens on the :Fingers slot. Close checks for pieces between the fingers when closing the gripper, and, if there is a piece, computes new fillers for :PieceHeld, :HeldPosition, and :PalmClearance. A piece, when grasped by the gripper, has its :Support and :SupportSurface slots set to NIL.

(2) The Open procedure opens the gripper fingers as far as possible (as given by :MaxSpread), making changes similar to those made by the Close procedure. If :PieceHeld is non-NIL, opening the gripper fingers results in dropping the piece. A dropped piece has its :Support and :SupportSurface fillers recomputed.

(3) The Translate procedure computes a new filler for :Position reflecting a translation of a given number of units along a given axis from the current value of :Position.

(4) The Rotate procedure computes a new filler for :Position reflecting a rotation of a given number of units along a given axis from the current value of :Position.

(5) The MoveTo procedure resets the :Position filler to a given new position.

(6) The NewToken procedure is not used by the emulator, but rather is invoked automatically for every new token of this type to initialize certain slot fillers. NewToken is also responsible for setting up the graphics display of the $Arm token (much like

$Piece.NewToken).

(7) The Render procedure is used to project the 3D wireframe in the :DisplayOps into a 2D representation stored in the $Segment token, taking into account the current position of the piece and all of the viewing parameters of the current view (see Section 6.4.1).

There are two if-changed procedures attached to slots on tokens of type $Arm. These procedures are used to model arm/piece interactions.

(1) Changing the robot arm's position must modify the position of any piece currently held by the arm. This is handled by an if-changed procedure attached to the arm's :Position slot. When the :Position is changed and the :PieceHeld filler is non-NIL, a new :Position value for the :PieceHeld filler is computed using the arm's new :Position and the :HeldPosition filler on $Arm.

(2) Changing the robot arm's finger spread also invokes an if-changed procedure attached to the :Spread slot of $Arm. If the value of spread is changed (by a Close or Open request) the following procedure is invoked:

```
If old :Spread is equal to :MaxSpread
    then if :Position is Inside? any piece in :Contents of :WorkSpace
        then set :Spread, :Contacts, :PieceHeld and :HeldPosition
        else set :Spread to 0 and :PieceHeld to NIL
    else if :PieceHeld is not NIL
        then drop :PieceHeld and establish its support
            in :WorkSpace and set :PieceHeld to NIL.
```

6.4. Implementing the Graphics Subsystem

The graphics system implementation consists of two types, $View and $Segment, interfaced to the modeler via an if-changed procedure attached to the :Position slot of each $Piece token. The graphics package is not meant in any way to represent the state of the art in computer graphics. Its description is included only for completeness. The reader is referred to [63] for a more thorough discussion of computer graphics.

6.4.1. $View

A view maps a three-dimensional wireframe representation of the workspace collected from the :DisplayOps slots of the pieces contained in

Table 6.14
$View

Supers	LazyCopy	
TypeSlots	::LazySlots	:Segments, :WorkSpace
Slots	:WorkSpace	pointer to workspace being viewed
	:Window	pointer to window on screen
	:Segments	list of segments for this view
	:DrawOp	one of PAINT, INVERT, ERASE
	:EraseOp	one of PAINT, INVERT, ERASE
	:ViewPoint	observer position
	:ViewWidth	width of view in window
	:ViewHeight	height of view in window
	:ViewingTransform	projection transform
Procedures	AddPiece	add piece to view
	NewToken	initialize view
	Redraw	recompute all segments
	Refresh	replot the view
	SetView	calculate projection transformation

the workspace (as well as the robot arm) onto a two-dimensional window on the workspace screen. It is a subtype of $LazyCopy, since we want the view to track the changes made over time by the history mechanism.

The type $View (see Table 6.14) contains slots which are mostly used to contain the view's *viewing parameters*.

(1) The :WorkSpace slot points to the workspace snapshot represented by this view.

(2) The :Window slot points to the INTERLISP-D window used for display of the workspace.

(3) The :Segments slot contains a list of tokens of type $Segment, one for each piece to be rendered. In addition, one segment token is used to represent the robot arm.

(4) The :DrawOp slot contains the INTERLISP-D display operation to be used for drawing pieces in the window. This is initially set to PAINT.

(5) The :EraseOp slot contains the INTERLISP-D display operation to be used for erasing pieces in the window. This is initially set to

ERASE.

(6) The :ViewPoint slot contains a matrix specifying the position of the viewer (or camera). Recall from our discussion of Section 4.2.1.1 that the viewpoint and the workspace must occupy distinct halfspaces.

(7) The :ViewWidth slot contains an integer describing how much of the workspace's width is mapped onto the window.

(8) The :ViewHeight slot contains an integer describing how much of the workspace's height is mapped onto the window.

(9) The :ViewingTransform slot contains the homogeneous coordinate matrix used to transform a point in three-space into a point in two-space. The :ViewingTransform is computed as a function of :ViewPoint, :ViewWidth, and :ViewHeight and need not be recomputed unless one of these fillers is changed.

The procedures attached to $View manipulate these slots.

(1) The AddPiece procedure adds a piece to the view. It creates a token of type $Segment to represent the piece, and adds it to the :Segments slot. It the displays the piece on the view by issuing an Update request to the segment token. In addition, :Position slot on the piece is tagged with an if-changed procedure so that any future changes made to the piece's position also issue an Update request to that piece's segment (for the robot arm, a similar if-changed procedure is also attached to the :FingerSpread slot).

(2) The NewToken procedure initializes the view by first creating a window on the workstation screen, and then invoking the SetView procedure to set up the viewing parameters.

(3) The Redraw procedure erases the window and issues an Update request to every segment in the :Segments filler. This causes the projection of each piece (as well as the robot arm) to be recomputed and redisplayed.

(4) The Refresh procedure erases the window and issues a Draw request to every segment in the :Segments filler. This causes the view to be redisplayed using the current piece projections.

(5) The SetView procedure is invoked to compute the :ViewingTransform filler from :ViewPoint, :ViewWidth, and :ViewHeight. The :ViewingTransform, when postmultiplied with a matrix representing a point in the workspace halfspace, results in a point on the plane separating the workspace halfspace and the viewer halfspace. The resulting point is the two-dimensional representation of the three-dimensional point as seen by the

camera located at the :ViewPoint.

6.4.2. $Segment

A segment contains the drawing commands, given as INTERLISP-D operations specific to the screen operations on the workstation, used to render a piece on a given view. Each segment corresponds to one and only one piece. When the piece is moved, it is necessary to recompute the drawing commands that render the piece on the view.

The slots on $Segment (see Table 6.15) are straightforward:

(1) The :Piece slot points to the piece rendered by this segment. The filler of :Piece is a token of type $Piece or a $LazyCopy of such a token.

(2) The :View slot points to the view on which to render the piece.

(3) The :DrawVersion slot contains a list of INTERLISP-D operations which, when executed, draw the wireframe of :Piece in :View.

(4) The :EraseVersion slot contains a list of INTERLISP-D operations which, when executed, erase the wireframe of :Piece in :View. The value of this slot is derived from :DrawVersion by a simple substitution of the draw operation for an erase operation in the INTERLISP-D statements.

The procedures attached to $Segment are also quite straightforward:

(1) The Draw procedure executes the INTERLISP-D operations listed on the :DrawVersion slot.

<table>
<tr><td colspan="3" align="center">Table 6.15
$Segment</td></tr>
<tr><td>*Supers*</td><td>LazyCopy</td><td></td></tr>
<tr><td>*TypeSlots*</td><td>::LazySlots</td><td>:Piece, :View</td></tr>
<tr><td>*Slots*</td><td>:Piece
:View
:DrawVersion
:EraseVersion</td><td>pointer to piece represented by segment
pointer to current view
line drawing operations
line erasing operations</td></tr>
<tr><td>*Procedures*</td><td>Draw
Erase
Update</td><td>execute :DrawVersion
execute :EraseVersion
recompute, erase, and redraw</td></tr>
</table>

(2)   The Erase procedure executes the INTERLISP-D operations listed on the :EraseVersion slot.

(3)   The Update procedure computes a new filler for :DrawVersion by issuing a Render request to the filler of :Piece. It then erases the existing view of the piece by issuing an Erase request, followed by redrawing the new version of the piece by issuing a Draw request. Finally, Update derives a new filler for :EraseVersion from the current filler of :DrawVersion. Update in effect provides a way of buffering the erase and draw operations so that the time spent computing the new view of a piece is not noticeable to the person viewing it. Note that Update relies on the current value of the :ViewingTransform slot of the view.

6.5. Implementing the Schema System

In this section, we describe the implementation of the ARMS schema system described in Section 5.1. Appendix F contains capsule summaries of all of the schemata initially built into the ARMS schema library.

6.5.1. $Schema

Our implementation represents schemata as tokens of various types. All of the schemata in the system are subtypes of the abstract type $Schema (see Table 6.16). $Schema implements some of the more general manipulation facilities for schemata. It is never directly instantiated, but permits other schema types below it in the hierarchy to inherit its slots and procedures. It has the following procedures:

Table 6.16 $Schema		
Slots	:Episode	pointer to database
	:PrintName	character string label
Procedures	Fillers?	returns list of fillers
	Template?	returns a template
	CloneBySlot?	returns a list of clones
	ReconcileRequest?	reconciles self with target
	CloneAndReconcile?	reconciles clones with targets

(1)   The Filler? procedure returns a list of all of the fillers for this particular token.

(2)   The Template? procedure takes a single argument, the requester (another token), and returns a template that describes self in terms of the requester. The header of the template is simply the type of self. Template? scans the slots of both tokens and looks for matches between the bindings to return (along with the header) as the new template.

(3)   The CloneBySlot? procedure takes a slot name and a list of new fillers and returns a list of *clones* differing only in the filler of the named slot. Two schema tokens are clones if they are of the same type and differ only by one filler. For n fillers, it creates n-1 new clones: the remaining value is assigned as the filler for slot in self.

(4)   The ReconcileRequest? procedure takes a template and target schema token as arguments. The target schema represents the template as evaluated with respect to self. ReconcileRequest maps fillers back from the target schema token across the template to self.

(5)   The CloneAndReconcile? procedure takes a template and a list of target schema tokens as arguments. It is an extension of the ReconcileRequest procedure that handles multiple target schemata. It returns a list of clones of self which have been reconciled across the template with the list of target schemata.

6.5.2. $StateSchema

A $StateSchema (see Table 6.17) describes a relation in the physical world. Each state has a set of type slots that relates a particular token instantiation to other states and operators.

(1)   The ::Contradictions type slot contains a list of state schema templates describing other states which, if valid, negate the validity of self.

(2)   The ::Substantiators type slot contains a list of state schema templates describing other states which, if valid, support the validity of self.

(3)   The ::Constraints type slot contains a list of constraint schema templates describing constraints which, if valid, support the validity of self.

(4)   The ::Plans type slot contains a list of operator schema templates describing operators that could be used to achieve self.

Table 6.17 $StateSchema		
Supers	$Schema $MatchMixin	
TypeSlots	::MatchSlots ::Contradictions ::Substantiators ::Plans ::AntiPlans ::Constraints	schema templates schema templates schema templates schema templates schema templates
Slots	:StartTime :EndTime :Constraints :Substantiators :Enables :Supports :ExplainedBy	first known valid time last known valid time schema tokens schema tokens schema tokens schema tokens schema tokens
Procedures	Valid? Confirm? Establish? Contradict? Constraints? Substantiate? ExtendLeft? ExtendRight? Plan? AntiPlan? Realize? RealizeConstraints? Collect?	database: determines self's validity database: extends self's validity database: establishes unique self database: checks for contradictions database: checks for constraints database: checks for supporters database: extends validity back in time database: extends validity forward in time planner: plans to achieve self planner: plans to override self planner: completes slots of self planner: completes slots of self generalizer: returns subtree below

(5) The ::AntiPlans type slot contains a list of operator schema templates describing operators that could be used to override the validity of self.

Each of these type slots is initialized to NIL on $StateSchema. Each individual subtype of $StateSchema will have its own filler for these type slots.

In addition to these type slots, each schema contains a minimal set of token slots which, when bound, describe the particular instance of the state represented by a given token.

(1)   The :StartTime slot contains a number indicating the earliest known time tick where self is valid. It is set by the state schema database.

(2)   The :EndTime slot contains the latest known time tick where self is valid. It is set by the state schema database.

(3)   The :Enables slot is used by both the understander and planner to represent operator schema tokens requiring self as a precondition. These tokens correspond to the template on the ::Enables type slot.

(4)   The :Supports slot is used by both the understander and planner to represent operator schema tokens pointing to self as a subgoal. These tokens correspond to the template on the ::Supports type slot.

(5)   The :ExplainedBy slot is used by both the understander and planner to represent operator schema tokens pointing to self as a goal. These tokens correspond to the template on the ::ExplainedBy type slot.

(6)   In addition to these generic state schema token slots, each subtype of $StateSchema contains a set of token slots particular to the semantics of the state. For example, to represent the relation:

   $Peg1 rests on top of $Washer1

   (as was the case in the observed example of Chapter 2) we use a token $Stacked1 of type $Stacked with appropriate slots bound to both descriptors $Peg1 and $Washer1. When $Peg1 is later stacked on top of $Block1, we instantiate another token of type $Stacked, but with different bindings for the slots.

The $StateSchema type has the following procedures attached to it:

(1)   The Establish? procedure is the heart of the database mechanism. Establish? takes a state schema token and adds it to the database if the token is valid and unique. Validity is determined using the Valid?, Contradict?, Substantiate? and Constraints? procedures. Uniqueness is enforced by examining possible matches in the database and returning a pointer to either the state schema token given as an argument or the matching extant token found in the database.

(2)   The Valid? procedure is unique to every subtype of $StateSchema. It performs the geometric reasoning necessary to determine whether self is valid at the given time. Valid? is responsible for

filling in the unbound slots peculiar to a given state schema during the understanding process.

(3) The Confirm? procedure is also unique to every subtype of $StateSchema. It performs the geometric reasoning necessary to determine whether self persists unchanged over adjacent time ticks. Confirm? usually requires much less computation than Valid?: it may, for example, simply check that the pieces involved in the relation represented by self remain unmoved.

(4) The Constraints? procedure queries the database for every template on ::Constraints. If every template is valid, the corresponding tokens are placed on the :Constraints slot and the procedure returns self. Otherwise, the procedure returns NIL. Constraints? is inherited from $StateSchema.

(5) The Contradict? procedure queries the database for every template on ::Contradictions. If none of the templates are valid, the procedure returns self. Otherwise, the procedure returns NIL. Contradict? is inherited from $StateSchema.

(6) The Substantiate? procedure queries the database for every template on ::Substantiators. If every template is valid, the corresponding tokens are placed on the :Substantiators slot and the procedure returns self. Otherwise, the procedure returns NIL. Substantiate? is inherited from $StateSchema.

(7) The Collect? procedure is used by the generalizer to explore the causal model. If one considers the causal model to be a tree rooted at the goal state, the Collect? procedure returns subtrees of the causal model as rooted at self. Collect? takes an argument specifying the format of the subtree returned. Collect? traverses links established by the :Substantiators, :Enables, :ExplainedBy, and :Supports slots.

(8) The Plan? procedure is used by the planner. It refers to the ::Plans type slot for possible ways of achieving self as a goal. The templates on ::Plans indicate operator schemata that achieve this state as a goal. Plan? is inherited from $StateSchema.

(9) The AntiPlan? procedure is also used by the planner. It refers to the ::AntiPlans type slot for possible ways of overriding self as a goal. The templates on ::AntiPlans indicate operator schemata that have at least one of the contradictions of this state as a goal, thus overriding the validity of the state. AntiPlan? is inherited from $StateSchema.

(10) The RealizeConstraints? procedure is used by the planner to flesh out the unbound slots in self during planning. RealizeConstraints?

uses the constraint schema templates on ::Constraints, along with the known slot fillers, in order to derive fillers for some of the unbound slots.

(11) The Realize? procedure is also used by the planner to complete the fillers on incompletely specified state tokens. Realize? is unique to every state schema; it is therefore responsible for fleshing out the slots peculiar to self during the planning process in much the same way Valid? is used during the understanding process.

(12) The ExtendLeft? procedure attempts to extend the validity of the state token back in time from the current value of :StartTime. It invokes the Confirm? procedure with decreasing values of time until it fails or reaches time 0. ExtendLeft? updates the value of :StartTime.

(13) The ExtendRight? procedure attempts to extend the validity of the state token forward in time from the current value of :EndTime. It invokes the Confirm? procedure with increasing values of time until it fails or reaches the current time. ExtendRight? updates the value of :EndTime.

6.5.2.1. $ConstraintSchema

The definition of $ConstraintSchema (see Table 6.18) parallels that of $StateSchema. A constraint has a fixed slot set as described in Section 5.1.1.1.1.

(1) The :Type slot indicates what relation must be satisfied between the other slots in order for this constraint to be valid. This is either a unary or a binary relation, such as LESSP (integer less than) or EQP (integer equals).

(2) The :Path1 slot is used to describe the first argument to the relation given as the filler of :Type. A path corresponds to a slot name or a sequence of slot names to be followed as pointers from the requesting schema.

(3) The :Path2 slot is used (if present) to describe the second argument to the relation given as the filler of :Type.

(4) The :Constant slot is a pointer that is to be used (if present) as the second argument to the relation given as the filler of :Type. If :Path2 is not given, :Constant must be given. If :Path2 is given, :Constant may be left unfilled. If both :Path2 and :Constant are given, then :Path2 is used to determine the second argument, and the result from the evaluation of the relation given in :Type is checked for equality with the filler of :Constant.

Table 6.18 $ConstraintSchema		
Supers	$Schema $MatchMixin	
TypeSlots	::MatchSlots	
Slots	:Enables :Type :Path1 :Path2 :Constant :Templates	list of state schema tokens binary relation or request path to argument 1 path to argument 2 (optional) value for argument 2 (optional) list of template indexed by requester
Procedures	Valid? Establish? Template?	database: determines validity of self database: establishes unique self returns a template for requester

Recall also that a constraint schema does not change with time. Therefore the Establish? and Valid? procedures, which are used by the database mechanism, are slightly different from those for $StateSchema.

Note the absence of a Confirm? procedure, since once a constraint is deemed valid there is no need to confirm it for differing time values.

The Template? procedure is also slightly different from the $Schema.Template? procedure. Since a constraint often evaluates to something like:

5 is greater than 2,

it is important to retain the original form of the constraint template with respect to the requesting schema. In other words, if schema Ai$ requests a constraint template

($C (Type LESSP)(Path1 :Width)(Constant 5))

an entry of the form

(Ai$. ($C (Type LESSP)(Path1 :Width)(Constant 5)))

is retained on the :Template slot. This entry permits the reconstruction of the particular constraint template corresponding to this constraint schema token. Note that different constraint templates may end up pointing to the same constraint schema token, since, of course, 5 is always greater than 2. The Template? procedure simply accesses :Template using the requesting schema as an index and returns the corresponding entry.

6.5.2.2. $JointSchema

The abstract type $JointSchema (see Table 6.19) and its subtypes implement the ARMS domain theory. Recall from our discussion of Sections 4.1.5 and 5.1.1.1.2 that a joint relates two primitives (and hence two pieces) by describing a family of legal transformations between them. These transformations are given as sets of degrees of freedom between the joint's end piece/primitive pairs.

Two totally unrelated pieces in free space have six degrees of freedom between them. Three of the degrees of freedom are orthogonal prismatic degrees of freedom. These permit the repositioning of one piece with respect to the other by sliding it along the X, Y, and/or Z axes of some coordinate frame of reference. The other three degrees of freedom (remember there are a total of six for unrelated pieces) are revolute degrees of freedom. These permit the reorientation of one piece with respect to the other by twisting it around the X, Y, and/or Z axes of the coordinate frame of reference.

The immediate subtypes of $JointSchema comprise the abstract joint schemata, while their subtypes in turn comprise the physical joint schemata. Abstract joint schemata describe the mechanical behavior of the joint, while physical joint schemata describe the physical realization of the joint.

The implementation of $JointSchema roughly parallels that of $StateSchema, with a few additions and slight modifications. $JointSchema contains a set of type slots which, in addition to the type slots inherited from $StateSchema, relate a particular token instantiation to other states and operators.

(1) The ::InstantiationType type slot is used to mark a particular instantiation as a simple or compound joint. A simple joint relates its piece/primitive pairs directly, while a compound joint relates its piece/primitive pairs via a chain of subjoints. ::InstantiationType is NIL for a simple joint, while for on a compound joint it contains a list of slot names where the interim pieces and primitives are stored.

(2) The ::InstantiationSubstantiators type slot contains a set of state schema templates which, when instantiated and valid, imply this joint is also valid. ::InstantiationSubstantiators are only used for physical joint schemata.

(3) The ::InstantiationConstraints type slot contains a set of constraint schema templates describing the interpiece physical constraints

	Table 6.19 $JointSchema	
Supers	$StateSchema $MatchMixin	

TypeSlots	::MatchSlots
	::InstantiationType
	::InstantiationConstraints
	::InstantiationSubstantiators
	
	::DOFs
	
	::DOFConstraints
		
		simple or compound joint
		interpiece constraints
		substantiators for physical
		  joint schemata
		degree of freedom
		  templates
		interDOF constraints

Slots	:Pieces
	:Transform
	
	:InstantiationConstraints
	:DOFSlots
	
	:DOFConstraints
		list of pieces in joint
		current relation between
		  end pieces
		constraint schema tokens
		slot names for degree
		  of freedom tokens
		constraint schema tokens

Procedures	BuildNewJointSchema
	
	Confirm?
	DOFRealize?
	DOFValid?
	
	KnownJointInstantiation?
	
	NewJointInstantiation?
	
	Plan?
	Realize?
	RealizeInstantiations?
	Valid?
	
	VerifyConstraints?
	
	VerifySubstantiators?
		verifier: adds new
		  physical joint schema
		database: confirms validity
		planner: completes slots
		database: check validity of
		  degrees of freedom
		database: known physical
		  joint schema
		database: find kinematic
		  chain equivalent
		planner: achieves self
		planner: completes slots
		planner: completes slots
		database: determines
		  validity of self
		database: checks
		  constraints
		database: checks
		  substantiators

that must be true for the joint to be valid. ::InstantiationConstraints are only used for physical joint schemata.

(4) The ::DOFs type slot contains a list of degree of freedom templates that describe the degrees of freedom which characterize this particular joint instantiation.

(5) The ::DOFConstraints type slot contains a list of constraint schema templates that must be true for this joint to be valid. These constraint schema templates relate to the degrees of freedom which characterize this joint.

Each of these type slots is initialized to NIL on $JointSchema. Each individual subtype of $JointSchema will have its own fillers for these type slots.

(1) The :Pieces slot contains a list of pieces related by this joint. At the very least, :Pieces will contains pointers to the two end pieces of the joint. For compound joints, any interim pieces will also be included on :Pieces.

(2) The :Transform slot contains a matrix indicating the current position of the second joint end piece from the first joint end piece/primitive pair's frame of reference.

(3) The :InstantiationConstraints slot contains pointers to the instantiated versions of the constraint templates found on the ::InstantiationConstraints type slot.

(4) The :DOFSlots slot lists the slot names on self where pointers to the degree of freedom tokens characterizing self can be found.

(5) The :DOFConstraints slot contains pointers to the instantiated versions of the constraint templates found on the ::DOFConstraints type slot.

(6) In addition to these generic joint schema token slots, each immediate subtype of $JointSchema contains a set of token slots identifying the pieces and primitives involved in the joint. At the very least, these slots include :Piece1, :Piece2, :Primitive1, and :Primitive2 that describe the end piece/primitive pairs for the joint. Any interim piece/primitive pairs in the chain will appear as slots of the form :InterimPiece$i$ and :InterimPrimitive$j$.

The procedures attached to $JointSchema are inherited by all joint schemata, both physical joint schemata and abstract joint schemata. None of the subtypes of $JointSchema have any procedures attached to them at all.

(1)   The BuildNewJointSchema procedure takes a kinematic chain that corresponds to an abstract joint specification and creates a new subtype of the existing abstract joint schema. The new type is a physical joint schema describing how the abstract joint schema was achieved in the observed example. BuildNewJointSchema creates additional slots on the new type corresponding to any interim pieces and primitive in the kinematic chain.

(2)   The Confirm? procedure confirms the continued existence of the joint. If the relative positions of the pieces involved have not changed, the joint is easily confirmed. Otherwise, the substantiator set must be reestablished for the joint to be confirmed.

(3)   The DOFRealize? procedure creates the appropriate tokens of type $DegreeOfFreedom and returns self or a list of clones of self. DOFRealize? is analogous to $StateSchema.RealizeConstraints? in that it also applies the constraint templates on ::DOFConstraints as a filter on the returned set of clones.

(4)   The DOFValid? procedure establishes the appropriate tokens of type $DegreeOfFreedom for self and establishes their boundary conditions by issuing a FindBounds? request to each degree of freedom. In addition, DOFValid? checks for compliance to the constraint templates of ::DOFConstraints.

(5)   The KnownJointInstantiation? procedure is applied only to abstract joint schemata. It attempts to find a physical joint schema related to self that is valid at the current time. Physical joint schemata which implement self are found by examining subtypes of the type of self. KnownJointInstantiation? returns the first valid physical joint schema token that is an instantiation of a subtype of the type of self.

(6)   The NewJointInstantiation? procedure is applied only to abstract joint schemata when no known physical joint schema corresponding to self is found to be valid. It looks for an open kinematic chain relating the end piece/primitive pairs of self via some transitive chain of currently valid physical joint schemata.

(7)   The Plan? procedure is used by the planner. When applied to a physical joint schema, it follows the same procedure as $StateSchema.Plan?. When applied to an abstract joint schema, it issues a Plan? request to every possible realization of self as returned by a Realize? request.

(8)   The Realize? procedure is also used by the planner to complete the fillers on an incompletely specified joint schema token. Once the end piece/primitive pairs and any interim piece/primitive pairs are

fleshed out, Realize? issues a DOFRealize request to every degree of freedom if self is a physical joint schema. If self is an abstract joint schema, then Realize? issues a RealizeInstantiations? request. Realize? returns self, a list of clones of self, or NIL.

(9) The RealizeInstantiations? procedure returns all possible physical instantiations of the receiving abstract joint schema. It creates tokens corresponding to each subtype of the type of self, and issues a Realize? request to each resulting token. RealizeInstantiations? returns self, a list of clones of self, or NIL.

(10) The Valid? procedure ascertains the validity of both physical joint schemata and abstract joint schemata. When issued to a physical joint schema, Valid? returns self, a list of clones of self, or NIL. When issued to an abstract joint schemata, Valid? returns a token or list of tokens of the corresponding physical joint schemata or NIL. Valid? fleshes out all of the unfilled token slots on self. For physical joint schemata, it then issues VerifyConstraint? and VerifySubstantiator? requests, returning a value only if both complete successfully. If self is an abstract joint schema, Valid? first issues a KnownJointInstantiation? request, and, failing there, issues a NewJointInstantiation? request. Valid? returns a value only if one of these two requests returns a value.

(11) The VerifyConstraints? procedure checks the constraint templates on ::InstantiationConstraints for validity. It is only applied to physical joint schemata. Valid constraint schema tokens are placed on the token slot :InstantiationConstraints. This procedure returns self or NIL.

(12) The VerifySubstantiators? procedure checks the state schema templates on ::InstantiationSubstantiators for validity. It is only applied to physical joint schemata. Valid substantiator state schema tokens are placed on the :Substantiators token slot. In addition, VerifySubstantiators? issues a DOFValid? request to self. This procedure returns self or NIL.

6.5.2.2.1. $DegreeOfFreedom

The abstract type $DegreeOfFreedom (see Table 6.20) is used to represent a single degree of freedom of a given joint. Its function is to model the degree of freedom and its boundary conditions, determining the range of motion permitted by this particular physical instantiation.

$DegreeOfFreedom has the following token slots defined:

(1) The :Joint slot points to the joint schema this degree of freedom belongs to.

	Table 6.20 $DegreeOfFreedom	
Slots	:Joint	pointer to joint token
	:Piece1	joint end piece
	:Piece2	joint end piece
	:Primitive1	joint end primitive
	:Primitive2	joint end primitive
	:Orientation	major axis measured wrt :Primitive1
	:UpperBound	upper joint limit
	:UpperBoundType	upper joint limit
	:UpperStop	upper joint limit
	:LowerBound	lower joint limit
	:LowerBoundType	lower joint limit
	:LowerStop	lower joint limit
	:Range	range of travel between limits

(2) The :Piece1, :Piece2, :Primitive1, and :Primitive2 slots contain pointers to the end piece/primitive pairs of this joint.

(3) The :Orientation slot gives a matrix indicating the orientation of the degree of freedom major axis in the frame of reference of :Primitive1.

(4) The :UpperBound slot contains a matrix indicating the position of :Piece2 in the frame of reference of :Piece1 at the joint's upper limit of travel.

(5) The :UpperBoundType contains NIL if this is a soft bound (see Section 4.1); otherwise, it contains a pointer to a token representing the surface that imposes the hard bound.

(6) The :UpperStop slot contains a pointer to the other surface involved in the collision imposing the hard bound, or NIL if this is a soft bound.

(7) The :LowerBound, :LowerBoundType, and :LowerStop slots contain analogous information related to the joint's lower limit of travel.

(8) The :Range slot contains an integer indicating the range of travel available to the joint between its upper and lower limits of travel.

$DegreeOfFreedom has no procedures attached directly to it. Rather, there are procedures attached to the two subtypes of $DegreeOfFreedom that are used to represent the two distinct types of degrees of freedom described previously.

6.5.2.2.1.1. $PrismaticDOF, $RevoluteDOF

The types $PrismaticDOF and $RevoluteDOF (see Tables 6.21 and 6.22) are used to represent the two distinct types of degrees of freedom. They have no type or token slots, but only parallel sets of procedures attached to them.

(1)   The Cancel? procedure compares the :Range of self against a system-wide tolerance. If the range is reduced below the tolerance, the degree of freedom is no longer considered viable, and Cancel? returns T.

(2)   The FindBounds? procedure establishes lower and upper bounds (either soft or hard) for a degree of freedom. It also sets the :Range filler to reflect the range of travel available to the degree of freedom. FindBounds? works by looking for possible collisions between end pieces while moving one of them along the axis of the degree of freedom. FindBounds? also takes an optional pieceList argument that specifies other pieces to consider as possible collision agents. This allows establishing bounds on degrees of freedom within a kinematic chain, rather than simply on degrees

Table 6.21
$PrismaticDOF

Supers	$DegreeOfFreedom	
Procedures	Cancel?	compares :Range to tolerance
	FindBounds?	establishes bounds
	Matches?	matches degrees of freedom

Table 6.22
$RevoluteDOF

Supers	$DegreeOfFreedom	
Procedures	Cancel?	compares :Range to tolerance
	FindBounds?	establishes bounds
	Matches?	matches degrees of freedom

of freedom from a simple joint.

(3) The Matches? procedure mimics the $MatchMixin.Matches? procedure in its calling protocols. Note, however, that $DegreeOfFreedom is not a subtype of $MatchMixin: the local Matches? procedure is tailor-made for comparing degrees of freedom.

6.5.2.2.2. $CylindricalJoint

The type $CylindricalJoint (see Table 6.23) is fairly representative of the immediate subtypes of $JointSchema. As such, it was chosen as an example of an abstract joint schema. In general, an abstract joint schema will contain certain type slot values that make it differ from other abstract joint schemata. In this case, the relevant type slots are ::DOFs and ::Constraints, but other abstract joint schemata may specialize a different slot set.

Recall that a cylindrical joint has two degrees of freedom, a prismatic degree of freedom and a revolute degree of freedom, aligned on the same major axis. The type $CylindricalJoint has two type slots that override the corresponding type slot default values given in $JointSchema.

(1) The ::DOFs type slot contains two templates: one for a $PrismaticDOF and one for a $RevoluteDOF. The two degrees of freedom share a single :Orientation.

(2) The ::Constraints type slot contains constraint schema templates indicating that the two end pieces must be different, and that the two end primitives must belong to their respective end pieces.

Table 6.23
$CylindricalJoint

Supers	$JointSchema	
TypeSlots	::DOFs	degree of freedom templates
	::Constraints	constraint schema templates
Slots	:Piece1	joint end piece
	:Piece2	joint end piece
	:Primitive1	joint end primitive
	:Primitive2	joint end primitive
	:Orientation	major joint axis wrt :Primitive1

In addition, $CylindricalJoint contains the following token slots:

(1) The :Piece1, :Piece2, :Primitive1, and :Primitive2 slots contain pointers to the end piece/primitive pairs of this joint.

(2) The :Orientation slot gives a matrix indicating the orientation of both degrees of freedom in this joint based on the frame of reference of :Primitive1.

6.5.2.2.3. $RigidJointA

The type $RigidJointA (see Table 6.24) is fairly representative of the physical joint schemata built into the system. Recall that physical joint schemata may be acquired by the system in the course of a learning episode (see Section 5.3.2.1.2). As with abstract joint schemata, physical joint schemata in general contain a specialized set of type and token slots that are available only in their general form on $JointSchema. For $RigidJointA, the specialized type slots are the ::InstantiationSubstantiators and ::InstantiationConstraints.

Recall that a rigid joint has no degrees of freedom between its end piece/primitive pairs. The type $RigidJointA has two type slots that override the corresponding type slot default values given in $JointSchema.

(1) The ::InstantiationSubstantiators slot contains a single state schema template describing an $Inserted state schema.

(2) The ::InstantiationConstraints slot contains constraint schema templates which force :Primitive1 to be a CSG solid, while :Primitive2 must not be a CSG solid. In addition, a constraint is placed on the relative sizes of :Primitive1 and :Primitive2 so that insertion achieves a rigid fit.

Table 6.24
$RigidJointA

Supers	$RigidJoint	
TypeSlots	::InstantiationSubstantiators	substantiators for physical joint schemata
	::InstantiationConstraints	interpiece physical constraints

6.5.3. $OperatorSchema

All of the operator schemata in ARMS are subtypes of the type $OperatorSchema (see Table 6.25). An operator schema describes how some action or set of actions taken by the robot arm affect the world state. Each operator schema has a set of type slots that describe how a particular token instantiation is related to other states and operators.

(1) The ::Goals type slot contains a list of state schema templates describing states that result from the application of self.

(2) The ::Preconditions type slot contains a list of state schema templates describing state that must be valid in for self to be applied.

(3) The ::SubGoals type slot contains a list of state schema templates (possibly mixed with sublists of state schema templates) describing a partial ordering of states that characterize the application of self.

(4) The ::Body type slot contains a single operator schema template describing an operator which, when applied in the context

Table 6.25		
$OperatorSchema		
Supers	$Schema	
TypeSlots	::Goals	list of goal templates
	::Preconditions	list of precondition templates
	::SubGoals	list of subgoal templates
	::Body	body template
	::Suggestions	list of action schema templates
Slots	:Goals	list of goal instances
	:Preconditions	list of precondition instances
	:SubGoals	list of subgoal instances
	:Body	body instance
	:Suggests	list of action schema instances
Procedures	Activate?	understander: checks operator for activation
	Suggest?	understander: returns likely suggestions of self
	Execute?	planner: executes self as a plan
	Collect?	generalizer: returns subtree below self

established by the preconditions and subgoals of self, causes the goal states to become valid.

(5) The ::Suggests type slot contains a list of state schema templates describing states that should be considered for activation when self becomes active. Usually these suggested states contain self as their body.

Each of these type slots is initialized to NIL on $OperatorSchema. Each individual subtype of $OperatorSchema will have its own filler for these type slots.

In addition to these type slots, each schema contains a minimal set of token slots which, when bound, describe the particular instance of the state represented by a given token.

(1) The :Goals slot us used by both the understander and planner to represent state schema tokens resulting from the application of self. These tokens correspond to the templates on the ::Goals type slot.

(2) The :Preconditions slot is used by both the understander and planner to represent state schema tokens that must be valid for the application of self. These tokens correspond to the templates on the ::Preconditions type slot.

(3) The :SubGoals slot us used by both the understander and planner to represent a partial ordering of state schema tokens characterizing the application of self. These tokens correspond to the templates on the ::SubGoals type slot.

(4) The :Body slot us used by both the understander and planner to represent an operator schema token which, when applied in the context established by the preconditions and subgoals of self, results in the validity of the goals. This token corresponds to the template on the ::Body type slot.

(5) The :Suggests slot us used by both the understander and planner to represent state schema tokens that are suggested upon activating self. These tokens correspond to the templates on the ::Suggests type slot.

(6) In addition to these generic state schema token slots, each subtype of $OperatorSchema contains a set of token slots particular to the semantics of the operator. These slots generally correspond to the union of slots on the goal states of self.

Unlike the $StateSchema.Realize or $StateSchema.Valid? procedures, none of the procedures attached to $OperatorSchema are overridden by procedures tailor-made to suit a particular operator. The procedures attached to $OperatorSchema are applicable to all operator schema tokens (with the possible exception of the primitive operators: see next section).

(1)   The Activate? procedure determines whether the suggested schema represented by self is activated in the current context. Activate? implements the non-predictive understanding process of Section 5.3.1.3.2. Activate? returns NIL if the schema fails to meet the activation conditions. If the activation conditions are met, Activate? returns self or a list of clones of self, depending on whether self was fully instantiated. If the schema was only partially instantiated, the list of clones represents all active fully-instantiated versions of self.

(2)   The Suggest? procedure is used by the understander. Suggest? returns the list of operator schemata suggested by the activation of self. Suggest? instantiates the schema templates on the ::Suggests type slot of self and checks for validity of their goal states. Only suggestions whose goal states are valid at the current time are returned as the result of Suggest?.

(3)   The Execute? procedure is used by the planner. Execute? implements the execution step described in Section 5.2.2. Execute? returns self (or a clone of self) if the goals of self (or its clone) are successfully achieved (or are already valid).

(4)   The Collect? procedure is used by the generalizer to explore the causal model. If one considers the causal model to be a tree rooted at the goal state, the Collect? procedure returns subtrees of the causal model as rooted at self. Collect? takes an argument specifying the format of the subtree returned. Collect? traverses links established by the :Preconditions, :SubGoals, :Body, and :Goals slots.

6.5.3.1. $PrimitiveSchema

Primitive operator schemata are all subtypes of the abstract type $PrimitiveSchema (see Table 6.26). $PrimitiveSchema is in turn a subtype of $OperatorSchema. It contains the following additional slots:

(1)   The :Time slot contains a value giving the time tick this operator was executed.

(2)   The :Position slot contains a matrix giving the end position of the gripper, after command execution, for this primitive.

Table 6.26
$PrimitiveSchema

Supers	$OperatorSchema	
Slots	:Time	time of execution
	:Position	end gripper position
Procedures	Execute?	executes the primitive

The only procedure attached to $PrimitiveSchema is the Execute? procedure, which takes care of some of the bookkeeping involved in executing a primitive arm command. It is similar to the $OperatorSchema.Execute? procedure, but without the recursive execution of other operators.

Finally, we note that each of the five primitive arm commands is implemented as a subtype of $PrimitiveSchema. The individual primitive operator schemata also have individualized Execute? procedures that interface the schema system with the history mechanism by issuing an Input request to the current episode (see Section 6.6.2). Each individual Execute? procedure (e.g., $Open.Execute?, $MoveTo.Execute?) shares the bookkeeping facility of $PrimitiveSchema.Execute?.

6.6. Implementing the Top Level

This section describes the type $Episode (see Table 6.27), tokens of which are used to represent each learning or problem-solving episode. The performance element, the learning element, the emulator, the history mechanism, and the schema system database mechanisms are all implemented as procedures attached to this type.

We divide our discussion of the type $Episode along functional lines. We first discuss those slots and procedures that cannot be strongly identified with a single function of this type. We then proceed to describe the implementation of the history mechanism, the database, the planner, the understander, the verifier, and the generalizer.

6.6.1. General Description of $Episode

For every example, whether it be a learning or problem-solving example, a new token of type $Episode is created. For the scenario of Chapter 2 there would be multiple tokens: one corresponding to each learning or problem-solving episode. Every episode, regardless of whether a learning or problem-solving one, has a goal associated with it. Finally, each episode has a certain set of slots and procedures that

Table 6.27a		
$Episode		
Slots	:PlanMode	learning/planning episode
	:Goal	goal template specification
	:GoalSchema	pointer to goal token
	:AssemblySequence	series of robot arm command tokens
	:ActiveSchemas	active operator schemas
	:VerboseMode	diagnostic messages on/off
	:StatsFlag	statistics gathering on/off
	:OpGenFlag	generality/operationality tradeoff flag
	:Browser	pointer to causal model display
	:RS232Mode	output to real arm on/off
	:CurrentTime	history mechanism: time in clock ticks
	:WorkSpace	history mechanism: pointer to current snapshot
	:Trace	history mechanism: previous snapshots
	:OpenStates	database
	:RightOpenStates	database
	:LeftOpenStates	database
	:ClosedStates	database
	:ValidConstraints	database: valid constraint schemata
	:JointSchemas	database: valid joint schemata

	Table 6.27b **$Episode**	
Procedures	AddBrowser	adds causal model browser
	AddView	adds graphic display
	AnalyzeDependencies	generalizer: finds shared substructures
	AnalyzeJoints	generalizer: orders by DOF dependencies
	BreakDownStates	generalizer: eliminates shared substructures
	BuildNewSchema	generalizer: builds new operator schema
	CloseLeft	database: firms :StartTime on state schema token
	CloseRight	database: firms :EndTime on state schema token
	DeterminePreconditions	generalizer: finds preconditions
	FindChains?	verifier: invoked by joint schema validation
	Generalize	generalizer: entry point
	Input	history: entry point
	NewToken	initializes browser and graphics
	Observe	understander: entry point
	Plan	planner: entry point
	PromotePreconditions	generalizer: promotes to subgoals
	PromoteSlots	generalizer: collects new slots
	Revert	history: resets to earlier time
	Valid?	database: entry point
	Verify?	verifier: entry point
	WorkSpace?	history: returns pointer to snapshot

provide user interface and debugging functions.

The relevant slots of $Episode are

(1)   The :PlanMode slot identifies which type of episode the particular token represents. If T, it represents a problem-solving episode. If NIL, it represents a learning episode.

(2)   The :Goal slot contains a schema template describing the expert-specified goal state. This is usually an abstract joint schema

template.

(3)   The :GoalSchema slot contains a fully instantiated physical joint schema corresponding to the abstract joint schema template of the :Goal slot.

(4)   The :AssemblySequence slot contains a list of primitive operator schemata representing the robot arm command sequence observed or planned to this point.

(5)   The :ActiveSchema slot contains a list of operator schemata activate by the schema activation mechanism in a learning episode, or realized by the planning process in a problem-solving episode.

(6)   The :VerboseMode flag slot turns diagnostic messages from the database mechanism on or off.

(7)   The :StatsFlag slot turns on statistics gathering for performance evaluation (see Appendix E).

(8)   The :GenOpFlag slot contains the value of the generality/operationality trade-off flag described in Section 5.3.2.3.

(9)   The :Browser slot turns the dynamic causal model display browser on or off. In addition, it is possible to set :Browser so that the model is displayed only at the end of the observed episode.

(10) The :RS232Mode flag slot turns on echoing of primitive arm commands to the real robot arm via the RS232 serial port.

There are times when it is expeditious to run the system without either a graphic view or a browser, since these tend to slow the system down quite a bit. Therefore, there are two related debugging procedures:

(1)   The AddView procedure turns on the graphic output if the current episode does not already have a view on the world. It takes a single argument representing the time tick identifying the desired view. This permits the expert to run the system without paying the overhead associated with maintaining the view, yet still be able to inspect a view of the world on demand.

(2)   The AddBrowser procedure turns on the dynamic causal model display browser if the current episode does not already have one. Like AddView, this permits the expert to inspect the state of the causal model at any time tick on demand.

The NewToken procedure is executed whenever a new token of type $Episode is created. It performs various initialization functions required by the graphics and browser subsystems.

6.6.2. Implementing the History Mechanism

The job of the history mechanism is to maintain the workspace snapshots that trace the history of this episode. The general idea is to use the $LazyCopy mechanism to support a kind of layered copying where each layer corresponds to a time tick. The history mechanism provides indexing facilities (by tick) and also manages the emulator, which is used to compute new snapshots upon receipt of an arm command. The history mechanism is implemented as a collection of slots and procedures on $Episode.

The slots of $Episode used to implement the history mechanism are

(1) The :CurrentTime slot records the time corresponding to the current snapshot.

(2) The :WorkSpace slot always points to a token of type $WorkSpace or $LazyCopy (Section 6.3.2) that represents the state at time :CurrentTime.

(3) The :Trace slot contains the previous layers of the emulator, represented as previous generations of $LazyCopy and $WorkSpace tokens.

These slots are manipulated by a set of procedures, also attached to the type $Episode.

(1) The Input procedure pushes the current :WorkSpace on :Trace, increments the value of :CurrentTime by 1, and creates a new workspace lazy copy by issuing a Copy request to the last snapshot. The new workspace snapshot becomes the new filler for :WorkSpace, and is passed to the emulator for updating.

(2) The WorkSpace? procedure takes an integer as its only argument and returns a pointer to the snapshot corresponding to that time tick. If no argument is given, a pointer to the current filler of :WorkSpace is returned.

(3) The Revert procedure allows unwinding of the system state to a previous time by flushing the later layers of the emulator. This is especially useful when debugging, since it permits re-executing a particular arm command that may occur late in a sequence. Revert simply resets the :WorkSpace slot to the snapshot corresponding to the desired time, and removes any later snapshots from :Trace.

6.6.3. Implementing the State Schema Database

The state schema database is responsible for creating and maintaining the state schema representation of the world. It must be able to create new schema tokens, determine their validity and temporal scope, and satisfy requests for information about both new and existing state schema tokens. It is implemented using a collection of slots and procedures on the type $Episode.

The database is accessed via the procedure $Episode.Valid?. This procedure takes the following arguments:

(1) A state schema template or token which is the object of the request;

(2) A pointer to the schema token making the request;

(3) A time value indicating at what tick to check for validity;

(4) A flag indicating whether the requester expects the database to return all matches or only the first one found.

$Episode.Valid? returns a token, a list of tokens, or NIL, indicating no valid token was found to match the request. The basic procedure is

---

```
If the request is a template, create a token using the pointer to requester.
If the request is a constraint then
    If the request matches an entry in :ValidConstraints then
        Insure request is listed on :Templates of match and return match.
    Else evaluate constraint.
        If evaluated constraint is true then
            Add evaluated constraint to :ValidConstraints and return it.
        Else if it is not true return NIL.
Else if the request is not a constraint then
    If the request can be found in the cache then
        Return the match.
    Else attempt to establish the new state.
        If request can be established then
            Add established request to cache and return it.
        Else return NIL.
```

Attempts to establish a new token are handled by sending the token an Establish? request. This request is fielded by either $ConstraintSchema.Establish? or $StateSchema.Establish?, depending on the type of the token.

The four slots :OpenStates, :LeftOpenStates, :RightOpenStates, and :ClosedStates contain lists of state schema tokens used to implement the database cache mechanism. We describe the caching mechanism by first considering the implementation of a simpler caching strategy and then extending it to the more complex ARMS caching strategy.

Recall that each state token contains :StartTime and :EndTime fillers that describe the temporal scope of the state. A naive caching strategy can be implemented using two slots :OpenStates and :ClosedStates as follows:

(1)   Whenever a new state schema token $Si is validated at time t, determine the earliest tick at which $Si is valid by attempting to confirm $Si at each time tick counting down from t. This can be accomplished by issuing an ExtendLeft? request to $Si and setting :StartTime to the value returned. :EndTime is set to t.

(2)   The new token $Si is placed on the :OpenStates list, signifying that while its :StartTime is known, its :EndTime is not definite.

(3)   At every new time tick, attempt to extend the :EndTime of every token on the :OpenStates list by issuing an ExtendRight? request to each token. If a token cannot be extended, transfer it from the :OpenStates list to the :ClosedStates list. Tokens on :ClosedStates have their temporal scopes firmly delineated by their :StartTime and :EndTime slots.

While this is an adequate (and easy to implement) caching strategy, it wastes precious computational resources in attempting to extend the scope of every new state schema token back to the first time tick, as well as in extending the scope forward at each new time tick. A simple extension consists of invoking the forward extension process only on demand: e.g., when a database request at time t matches a state schema token on :OpenStates with an :EndTime of t-n. This kind of on-demand extension can result in a significant savings of computational resources, since many tokens, once established, are never accessed again.

Extending the temporal scope of every new state schema token as far back as possible is also a waste of resources. In addition, the cost associated with this extension grows with the length of the assembly sequence. We can extend the notion of on-demand extension to include extending the :StartTime of a token backwards. To do this, we split the :OpenStates and :ClosedStates lists into the four lists :ClosedStates, :OpenStates, :RightOpenStates, and :LeftOpenStates.

(1)   The :ClosedStates slot contains tokens whose temporal scope (as described by the :StartTime and :EndTime slots) is known to be

nonextendible.

(2)   The :OpenStates slot contains tokens whose temporal scope (as described by the :StartTime and :EndTime slots) is possibly extendible both backward and forward in time.

(3)   The :LeftOpenStates slot contains tokens whose temporal scope (as described by the :StartTime and :EndTime slots) is possibly extendible only backward in time.

(4)   The :RightOpenStates slot contains tokens whose temporal scope (as described by the :StartTime and :EndTime slots) is possibly extendible only forward in time.

Every new state schema token Si established at time t is placed initially on :OpenStates with both :StartTime and :EndTime slots set to time t. If the token matches a future database query, its temporal scope may be extended on demand, causing migration of the token from :OpenStates to either :LeftOpenStates or :RightOpenStates and, eventually, :ClosedStates. This migration is handled by the following two procedures attached to $Episode:

(1)   The CloseLeft procedure fixes the current left endpoint of its argument (a state schema token) as firm. Depending on the current placement of the state schema token, this procedure causes migration of the token to either :RightOpenStates or :ClosedStates.

(2)   The CloseRight procedure fixes the current right endpoint of its argument (a state schema token) as firm. Depending on the current placement of the state schema token, this procedure causes migration of the token to either :LeftOpenStates or :ClosedStates.

6.6.4. Implementing the Planner

The planner is invoked by creating a new token of type $Episode, initializing it, and issuing a Plan request. Initialization consists of setting :CurrentTime to 0, setting the expert's goal specification (an abstract joint schema template) on the :Goal slot, and placing a token of type $WorkSpace representing the initial problem-solving world on the :WorkSpace slot. :PlanMode is set to T.

The Plan procedure takes the expert's goal specification, an abstract joint schema template on the :Goal slot, instantiates it, and places it on the :GoalSchema slot. It then issues a Plan request to the instantiated abstract joint schema. The bulk of the computation is supported by the individual state and operator schemata Plan, Realize, and Execute procedures.

6.6.5. Implementing the Understander

The understander is invoked by creating a new token of type $Episode, initializing it, and issuing a Observe request. Initialization consists of setting :CurrentTime to 0, setting the user's goal specification (an abstract joint schema template) on the :Goal slot, and placing a token of type $WorkSpace representing the initial problem-solving world on the :WorkSpace slot. :PlanMode is set to NIL.

The Observe procedure takes as its lone argument a list of primitive robot arm commands. The commands are specified as a command name (e.g., Open, MoveTo, etc.) and whatever arguments fully describe the command (see Section 4.1.4). The Observe procedure proceeds as follows:

(1) Read the next command input and create a primitive operator schema token Pi$ to represent the input.

(2) Issue an Execute? request to Pi$ (recall that the Execute? procedure attached to each primitive operator type in turn issues an Input command to the episode's history mechanism).

(3) Issue a Suggest? request to Pi$ and initialize the suggested schema list to the result.

(4) If the suggested schema list is empty, go to Step 1.

(5) Pop the first suggested schema Sj$ off the suggested schema list and issue it an Activate? request.

(6) If the Activate? request returned NIL, go to Step 4.

(7) Place each clone of Sk$ returned from the Activate? request on :ActiveSchemas. Send each clone a Suggest? request and append the results to the suggested schema list. Go to Step 4.

When there are no longer any primitive arm command inputs left to be processed, the Observe procedure issues a Verify? request, invoking the verifier. If the verifier terminates successfully (e.g., a non-NIL value results from the Verify? request), then before terminating, the Observe procedure issues a Generalize request, invoking the generalizer.

6.6.6. Implementing the Verifier

The verifier is invoked when the Observe procedure issues a Verify? request. The Verify? procedure is in itself quite straightforward. It begins by checking if there is a physical joint schema token in the database that matches the expert's goal specification (the filler of the :Goal slot). If there is, then the goal was recognized during understanding (Case 1 of Section 5.3.2.1). This situation fails to meet the ARMS learning criteria, and, therefore, the verifier terminates returning NIL.

If no matching abstract joint schema is found in the database, Verify? issues a Valid? request to the database mechanism using the expert's goal specification (from :Goal) as the object of the request. Verify? sets the value of this Valid? request on the :GoalSchema slot and then returns it as its own value: hence, if the database mechanism returns NIL, Verify? will also return NIL (corresponding to Case 4 of Section 5.3.2.1).

The joint schema validation mechanism attempts to validate the request, perhaps creating a new physical joint schema in the process. This corresponds to Cases 2 and 3 of Section 5.3.2.1. If successful, it returns a physical joint schema token that corresponds to the expert's partially specified abstract joint schema.

Note that the joint schema validation procedure may, in the course of attempting to establish a new physical joint schema, issue a FindChains? request to the current episode. The FindChains? procedure takes as its arguments two piece/primitive sets, and returns all transitive physical joint schema relationships currently in the database which can be used to relate the two arguments.

6.6.7. Implementing the Generalizer

The generalizer is implemented as a collection of procedures attached to the type $Episode.

(1)   The AnalyzeDependencies procedure takes as its argument an ordered set of state schema tokens recognized by the understander and determines what shared substructures exist in the subtrees rooted at each state. It returns a new ordered set of states that has no shared substructures. Shared substructure is found by listing all of the substates in the subtrees rooted at each element of the input and finding their set intersections. AnalyzeDependencies relies on BreakDownStates to derive the shared-substructure free state set.

(2)   The AnalyzeJoints procedure takes an unordered set of physical joint schema tokens recognized by the understander and imposes an ordering based on an analysis of their degrees of freedom. AnalyzeJoints insures that any physical joint schema which restricts another physical joint schema's degree of freedom occurs before the affected joint schema. If schemata that are not joint schemata are included on the input list, they are passed through undisturbed.

(3)   The BreakDownStates procedure takes a tree of state and operator schema tokens (the explanation) and a set of shared state schema tokens as its arguments. BreakDownStates recursively descends the tree until it is free of shared states. As the recursion unwinds, BreakDownStates retains the set of state schema tokens that describes the original tree at the highest possible level of description free from elements of the shared state set.

(4)   The BuildNewSchema procedure constructs a new subtype of $OperatorSchema describing the newly acquired assembly technique and integrates it into the system (see Section 5.3.2.3). It takes two sets of state schema tokens (the precondition and the subgoal sets) as well as an operator schema token (the body) as arguments. BuildNewSchema constructs schema templates from its arguments (by issuing Template? requests to the individual tokens) and uses the templates to characterize the new operator schema.

(5)   The DeterminePreconditions procedure takes a set of state schema tokens recognized by the understander and returns a set of state schema tokens which are unexplained yet included in the explanation subtrees rooted at elements of the argument set. This constitutes the initial precondition set for the new schema.

(6)   The PromotePreconditions procedure takes a set of precondition state schema tokens (such as that produced by a DeterminePreconditions request) and attempts to promote these into subgoals of the new schema currently under construction. PromotePreconditions is invoked from BuildNewSchema and implements the precondition promotion procedure of Section 5.3.2.3.

(7)   The PromoteSlots procedure takes two sets of state schema tokens (a subgoal set and a precondition set), a goal schema token, and an operator schema token (the body) representing the newly constructed schema. It returns a set of new slots that must be added to the newly constructed schema in order to permit transfer of bindings among its arguments. PromoteSlots is invoked from BuildNewSchema and implements the slot promotion process of Section 5.3.2.3.

(8)   The Generalize procedure is the top-level entry point to the generalizer. It relies on the verifier placing a validated physical joint schema token on the :GoalSchema slot that corresponds with the expert's goal specification as stored on the :Goal slot.
The top-level subgoal set is computed by issuing an AnalyzeJoints request using the substantiator set of the :GoalSchema filler as the

argument. Then, depending on the value of the :GenOpFlag filler, an AnalyzeDependencies request is issued that transforms the top-level subgoal set into a new subgoal set without any shared substructures. If the more general new operator schema is desired, the AnalyzeDependencies request is not issued.

A precondition set for the new schema is computed by issuing a DeterminePreconditions request with the current subgoal set as its argument. Precondition promotion is attempted by issuing a PromotePreconditions request. The promotion precondition process may cause modification to both the subgoal set and the precondition set.

The body of the new schema is set to the achieving operator of the last subgoal in the subgoal set. The last element is then removed from the subgoal set.

At this point, Generalize has determined the structure of the new operator schema, and issues a BuildNewSchema request with the subgoal set, the body, and the precondition set as arguments. BuildNewSchema constructs the new operator schema type, adds it to the hierarchy, and constructs the appropriate ::Plans and ::Suggests links on other members of the schema library (see Section 5.3.2.5).

Chapter 7
Scenario Revisited

In this chapter we re-examine the same transcript of the ARMS system discussed in Chapter 2. Recall the problem was to construct a widget from the initial state shown in Figure 7.1. $BoredBlock1 is on the right, with its socket also facing towards the right. $Washer1 is in the foreground, with $Peg1 stacked on top of it. In addition, $Block1 is in the left rear part of the workspace.

The gripper is shown in its nest position as a two-fingered palm with the two (closed) fingers pointed downwards. The goal state is specified as a partially instantiated abstract joint schema:

$RevoluteJoint [Piece1 = $Washer1, Piece2 = $BoredBlock1].

A token $RevoluteJoint0122 that represents this abstract joint schema is instantiated.

7.1. Attempting to Solve the Problem

The performance element now takes over and attempts to produce a sequence of primitive operator schemata which, when executed, will produce a final state consistent with the goal specification. The first step of this process is the design phase of Section 5.2.1.

Recall the design phase attempts to produce a fully instantiated physical joint schema from the partially instantiated abstract joint schema derived from the goal specification. From the abstract joint schema $RevoluteJoint0122 we index those physical joint schemata that represent physical realizations of this mechanical behavior.

While the system possesses the abstract joint schema type $RevoluteJoint, it has no physical joint schemata that correspond to it. Therefore, the design phase terminates unsuccessfully, causing the performance element to abort.

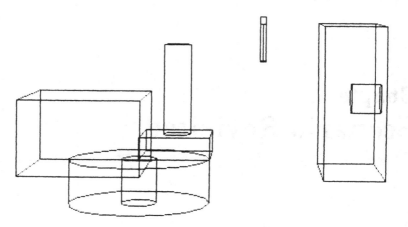

Initial State for Widget Assembly Problem

The disembodied robot arm gripper is located in the center of the picture with its fingers closed and pointing downwards. $BoredBlock1 is off to the right, with its socket also pointing to the right. $Block1 is in the left rear of the picture. $Peg1 is stacked on top of $Washer1 in the foreground, just left of center.

Figure 7.1

7.2. Observing the Expert's Plan

When the performance element gives up, control passes to the learning element, and the expert is asked to lead the robot arm through a solution. The expert's input is a list of 30 fully instantiated primitive operator schemata. As each input is read in, the emulator simulates the changing workspace by executing each arm command. Meanwhile, the understander constructs the causal model using the schema-activation mechanism described in Section 5.3.1.3.3.

Note that the solution presented by the expert contains several less-than-optimal subsequences. In particular,

(1)   Clearing $Peg1 off of the top of $Washer1 uses a sequence of four $Translate commands along the world coordinate system axes. There is no justification for using the four, more expensive, $Translate commands over a single $MoveTo.

(2) $Peg1 is stacked on top of $Block1 when it is removed from $Washer1. An optimal solution would not rely on the presence of the extraneous piece $Block1.

(3)   There is an extra $Rotate command before grasping $Washer1 which does not contribute to the success of the expert's plan.

Note that these subsequences do not affect the effectiveness of the solution. One would hope, however, that any operator schema acquired by the system that can be used to solve this problem would produce a better solution; i.e., one that doesn't rely on these quirks of the expert's plan.

7.3. Verifying the Solution

When the last input is read and the causal model is complete, the generalizer takes over. The first task of the generalizer is to ascertain that the final state actually fits the goal specification given by the expert.

In Section 5.3.2.1., we discussed the verification process and the four possible cases it must handle. The situation in this example is that of Case 3, i.e., there is no physical joint schema that can be used to justify the validity of the abstract joint schema given as the goal specification.

It is up to the verification process to construct some justification, on the basis of its naive kinematic domain theory, of how this assembly fulfills the function specified by the goal specification. The first step in this analysis is to look for a kinematic chain linking the two end pieces specified by the abstract joint $RevoluteJoint0122, the goal specification.

During the course of the understanding process, the system was able to recognize two physical joint schemata, $RigidJointA0301 and $CylindricalJointA0311. Recognition of these two joints was accomplished by the activation of two schemata $NewSchemaA0298 and $NewSchemaB0308. Both of these operator schemata are instantiations of operator schemata acquired by ARMS in the course of previous learning episodes.

These two recognized joints provide a chain between $Washer1 and $BoredBlock1 via $Peg1. In this case, this is the only extant kinematic chain between the desired end pieces.

The verifier now collects copies of all the degrees of freedom in the chain, recomputing all of their soft bounds by taking into account the presence of the other pieces in the chain. In this example, there are two degrees of freedom present: a prismatic degree of freedom and a revolute degree of freedom. Both are contributed by $CylindricalJointA0311.

The revolute degree of freedom from $CylindricalJointA0311 has no bounds, and no changes on the bounds are made by considering the other pieces in the kinematic chain. On the other hand, the prismatic degree of freedom contributed by $CylindricalJointA0311 suffers some modification when incorporated into the kinematic chain.

This prismatic degree of freedom currently has a hard bound imposed by a collision between the underside of $Peg1's head and the top surface of $Washer1. The other bound is a soft bound limited only by the length of the shaft of $Peg1. When the entire kinematic chain is considered, a collision between the underside of $Washer1 and the top surface of $BoredBlock1 causes the soft bound to become a hard bound. The range of motion remaining on the prismatic degree of freedom is so small as to fall below a system-wide tolerance value which indicates when a degree of freedom ceases to be significant.

The collected degrees of freedom of the kinematic chain are then mapped onto the expected degrees of freedom of the abstract joint schema $RevoluteJoint0122. In this case, the revolute degree of freedom corresponds to the single expected degree of freedom of $RevoluteJoint0122. The prismatic degree of freedom is canceled by the newly imposed bounds.

The verification process now constructs a new physical joint schema $RevoluteJointA, indexed by $RevoluteJoint, that represents this particular physical realization of joint function. The substantiator set for $RevoluteJointA contains $CylindricalJointA and $RigidJointA. Slots are created on $RevoluteJointA to permit mapping of fillers across the substantiator set, and constraints are added that reflect only those physical interrelations (e.g., shape and dimension relations) between the fillers that were crucial to the cancellation of the prismatic degree of freedom. An instance of the new schema, $RevoluteJointA0354, is created to represent the achieved goal state. Finally, new slots (e.g., InterimPiece1) representing internal chain pieces are added to the new physical joint schema. The verification process terminates successfully.

7.4. Generalizing the Solution

The top-level subgoal set of this episode consists of the substantiators of $RevoluteJointA0354, $CylindricalJointA0311 and $RigidJointA0301. From this subgoal set, the generalizer constructs a new operator schema to achieve the goal $RevoluteJointA, the newly added abstract schema corresponding to the current goal $RevoluteJointA0354.

The first step is to analyze any dependencies between these top-level subgoals in order to produce a partial ordering on the subgoal set. In this case, the analysis is simple since one of the two joints ($RigidJointA0301) imposes constraints on the degrees of freedom of the other joint ($CylindricalJointA0311). Hence, $CylindricalJointA0311 must be achieved before $RigidJointA0301.

At this point, the ARMS generalizer is capable of producing two different new operator schemata, depending on the value assigned to the current episode's generality/operationality trade-off flag (Section 5.3.2.3). This parameter reflects the level of representation chosen for the new schema: a more general new schema carries a higher price in planning, while a more operational new schema is applicable in fewer situations.

7.4.1. A More General New Schema

If we chose to produce the most general schema possible, the generalizer need not descend below this top-level subgoal set. In essence, the top-level subgoal set becomes the explanation for the observed episode.

Preconditions are collected from the top-level subgoal set members. The body of the new schema becomes the abstraction of $RigidJointA0301's achieving operator $NewSchemaA0298. The remaining subgoal becomes the only element of the new schema's subgoal set.

Slots are added to permit mapping fillers between the subgoal, body, and preconditions of the new schema. New slots are used to represent surfaces of InterimPiece1 and various important dimensions (e.g., length of the shaft, depth of the hole).

The new schema acquired is the most general representation of how this joint was achieved (see Figure 7.2). It essentially states

> To achieve an instance of $RevoluteJointA, achieve an instance of $CylindricalJointA between Piece1 of the joint and and another piece, InterimPiece1. Constrain the prismatic degree of freedom of the instance of $CylindricalJointA by achieving an instance of $RigidJointA between InterimPiece1 and Piece2 of the joint.

7.4.2. A More Operational New Schema

Examining this new schema reveals that much effort is being duplicated in any eventual expansion of the new schema undertaken by the performance element. For example, achieving $RigidJointA and $CylindricalJointA both require grasping InterimPiece1 ($Peg1 in this example). There should be no need to duplicate planning effort for this grasping operation.

This is the crucial insight that enables the production of a more operational new schema. If we descend the causal model until there are no more shared substructures and create a new schema at that level of representation (as opposed to the top level), we will have produced a more operational schema. This new schema is more operational since

```
((Supers OperatorSchema)
 (TypeSlots
  (Goals (($RevoluteJointA (Piece1 Piece1)
                           (Piece2 Piece2)
                           (Primitive1 Primitive1)
                           (Primitive2 Primitive2)
                           (Orientation Orientation)
                           (DOF1 DOF1)
                           (InterimPiece1 InterimPiece1)
                           (InterimPrimitive1 InterimPrimitive1)
                           (DOF2 DOF2))))
  (SubGoals (($CylindricalJointA (Piece1 InterimPiece1)
                                 (Piece2 Piece2)
                                 (Primitive1 InterimPrimitive1)
                                 (Primitive2 Primitive2)
                                 (Orientation Orientation)
                                 (DOF1 DOF1)
                                 (DOF2 DOF2))))
  (Body ($NewSchemaA (Piece1 InterimPiece1)
                     (Piece2 Piece1)
                     (Primitive1 InterimPrimitive1)
                     (Primitive2 Primitive1))))
 (TokenSlots
  (Piece1 NIL                   doc (* From goalSchema))
  (Piece2 NIL                   doc (* From goalSchema))
  (Primitive1 NIL               doc (* From goalSchema))
  (Primitive2 NIL               doc (* From goalSchema))
  (Orientation NIL              doc (* From goalSchema))
  (DOF1 NIL                     doc (* From goalSchema))
  (InterimPiece1 NIL            doc (* From goalSchema))
  (InterimPrimitive1 NIL        doc (* From goalSchema))
  (DOF2 NIL                     doc (* From goalSchema))))
```

More General Version of $NewSchemaC

Figure 7.2

there will not be any wasted planning effort during schema expansion and application.

The shared substructure analysis continues as described in Section 5.3.2.3. until the top-level subgoal set has been transformed into a new subgoal set with no interdependencies present between its members. The analysis is order-preserving: hence, the top-level subgoal set ordering imposed by the joint dependency analysis has carried through to the ordering of this new subgoal set as well.

Preconditions are collected from the members of the new subgoal set. The last element of the set is used to determine the body of the new schema. The remaining subgoals become the subgoals of the new schema.

The precondition promotion cycle is used to promote certain preconditions into the new subgoal set (see Section 5.3.2.3). In this example, all of the preconditions are promoted to the subgoal set. In addition, new slots are created (via the slot promotion process of Section 5.3.2.3) to permit the mapping of fillers among the elements of the new schema.

The schema produced, $NewSchemaC, is shown in Figure 7.3. It essentially states

> In order to achieve an instance of $RevoluteJointA, given the promoted precondition $Placed that describes the position of InterimPiece1, begin by achieving an instance of $BracedHoles for Piece1 and Piece2 of the joint. $Grasp InterimPiece1 from its $Placed position, carfully avoiding obstructing any surfaces of InterimPrimitive1, and achieve a $MultiAligned between InterimPrimitive1 and the previously braced holes. Finally, translate InterimPiece1 by a distance computed from the combined hole depth and the alignment offset.

How is this new schema less general than the schema produced in Section 7.4.1.? Suppose that the system is now shown a new strategy for constructing $RigidJoints and $CylindricalJoints. This new strategy would construct a $RigidJointA by first placing $Peg1 on its back with its shaft pointing up and then forcing $BoredBlock1 over it. The new schemata embodying this strategy would be indexed from the appropriate physical joint schemata, $RigidJointA and $CylindricalJointA: therefore, the more general new schema from Section 7.4.1. would immediately have access to this new strategy, while the more operational new schema would not.[22]

7.5. Solving the Same Problem After Learning

We now present the system with the same problem after schema acquisition, and give as a goal the partially specified abstract joint schema:

$RevoluteJoint [Piece1 = $Washer1, Piece2 = $BoredBlock1].

The design phase is responsible for fleshing out the abstract joint schema given as a goal specification and producing a corresponding physical joint schema.

A single token $RevoluteJointA0966 is returned by the design process. The new physical joint schema $RevoluteJointA was indexed from $RevoluteJoint. The $RevoluteJointA0966 schema contains pointers to all three pieces in the assembly rather than only the two

---

[22] For an empirical performance comparison, see Appendix E.

```
((Supers OperatorSchema)
 (TypeSlots
  (Goals (($RevoluteJointA (Piece1 Piece1)
                           (Piece2 Piece2)
                           (Primitive1 Primitive1)
                           (Primitive2 Primitive2)
                           (Orientation Orientation)
                           (DOF1 DOF1)
                           (InterimPiece1 InterimPiece1)
                           (InterimPrimitive1 InterimPrimitive1)
                           (DOF2 DOF2))))
  (SubGoals (((($Placed  (Piece InterimPiece1)
                         (SupportSurface NewSlot2)))
              ($BracedHoles  (Piece1 Piece2)
                             (Primitive1 Primitive2)
                             (Hole1 NewSlot3)
                             (Piece2 Piece1)
                             (Primitive2 Primitive1)
                             (Hole2 NewSlot4)
                             (Depth NewSlot5))
              ($Grasped (Piece InterimPiece1)
                        (OldSupportSurface NewSlot2)
                        (FreePrimitives InterimPrimitive1))
              ($MultiAligned (Piece1 InterimPiece1)
                             (Primitive1 InterimPrimitive1)
                             (Piece2 Piece2)
                             (Primitive2 Primitive2)
                             (Hole2 NewSlot3)
                             (Piece3 Piece1)
                             (Primitive3 Primitive1)
                             (Hole3 NewSlot4)
                             (Depth NewSlot5)
                             (Delta NewSlot1))))
  (Body ($FullMove  (Piece InterimPiece1)
                    (Delta NewSlot1))))
 (TokenSlots
  (Piece1 NIL                    doc (* From goalSchema))
  (Piece2 NIL                    doc (* From goalSchema))
  (Primitive1 NIL                doc (* From goalSchema))
  (Primitive2 NIL                doc (* From goalSchema))
  (Orientation NIL               doc (* From goalSchema))
  (DOF1 NIL                      doc (* From goalSchema))
  (InterimPiece1 NIL             doc (* From goalSchema))
  (InterimPrimitive1 NIL         doc (* From goalSchema))
  (DOF2 NIL                      doc (* From goalSchema))
  (NewSlot1 NIL                  doc (* Promoted slot))
  (NewSlot2 NIL                  doc (* Promoted slot))
  (NewSlot3 NIL                  doc (* Promoted slot))
  (NewSlot4 NIL                  doc (* Promoted slot))
  (NewSlot5 NIL                  doc (* Promoted slot))
```

More Operational Version of $NewSchemaC

Figure 7.3

mentioned in the goal specification.

Selection of the third piece to fill the InterimPiece1 slot is made in accordance with the constraints on the $RevoluteJointA schema. Recall these constraints were imposed on the basis of interpiece relations which were crucially true in the joint analysis. In this case, such constraints mandate, among other things, that the shaft size of InterimPiece1 match the diameter of the hole in $BoredBlock1 and be slightly smaller than the diameter of the hole in $Washer1.

Since there are only two pieces ($Block1 and $Peg1) in the initial state not already included in the goal specification, both are tested for conformance with the constraint set. $Peg1 is the only piece that can be used to fill the role of InterimPiece1.

Upon successful termination of the design phase, the planner proceeds to expand the plan embodied in $NewSchemaC. It indexes $NewSchemaC from the goal state $RevoluteJointA0966 produced by the design process. A new instance $NewSchemaC0971 is created and recursive applications of the plan and execution steps (described in Section 5.2.2) are performed.

The operator sequence produced by the more operational version of $NewSchemaC had 24 steps, which roughly correspond to

(1)   Brace $BoredBlock1 such that its hole is pointing upwards.

(2)   Clear $Peg1 off of $Washer1, placing it directly on the workspace surface in some free spot.

(3)   Grasp $Washer1 and stack it on top of $BoredBlock1 with holes aligned.

(4)   Grasp $Peg1 in such a way so as not to occlude the shaft, and align it with the holes in $Washer1 and $BoredBlock1.

(5)   Translate $Peg1 along the negative z-axis a distance corresponding to the alignment offset plus the minimum of either the $Peg1 shaft length or the combined $Washer1/$BoredBlock1 hole depth.

Note that, unlike the observed plan, the resulting operator sequence does not rely on the presence of $Block1. In addition, extraneous commands in the observed plan that do not figure in the explanation from which $NewSchemaC was derived do not occur in the system's plan.

7.6. Solving Similar Problems After Learning

$NewSchemaC can be applied in other problem situations to produce a successful assembly sequence. As long as the goal specification can be realized as an instance of $RevoluteJointA, $NewSchemaC may well be applicable.

In Appendix E, the performance of the ARMS system when planning $RevoluteJointA-type assemblies from various initial states and using various piece sets is examined. For the initial states of Figures 7.4 and 7.5, the goal specification remains the same:

$RevoluteJoint [Piece1 = $Washer1, Piece2 = $BoredBlock1].

For the initial state of Figure 7.4, the performance element produces a 12 step assembly sequence, while for that of Figure 7.5 30 steps were generated.

A more interesting example is shown in Figure 7.6. In this case, the goal specification was given as:

$RevoluteJoint [Piece1 = $Washer3, Piece2 = $BoredCylinder1].

Note that the desired assembly has quite a different physical aspect than that of the widget in the learning episode. Functionally, however, the structure demonstrates exactly the same joint behavior.

The design phase properly selects $Peg2 over $Peg1 to fill the role of InterimPiece1. This selection is based on the interpiece constraints associated with $RevoluteJointA. The planning phase produces an assembly sequence of 18 steps that achieves the goal specification.

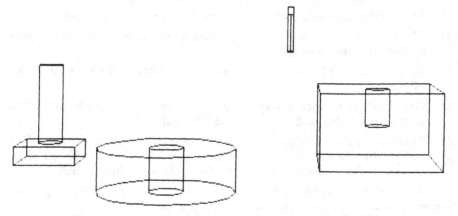

First Alternate Initial State for Widget Assembly Problem

The robot gripper is located in the center of the picture with fingers closed. $BoredBlock1 is to the right, $Peg1 is to the left, and $Washer1 is in the foreground just left of center.

Figure 7.4

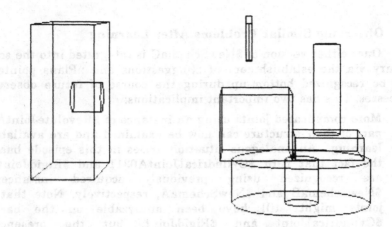

Second Alternate Initial State for Widget Assembly Problem

The robot gripper is located in the center of the picture with fingers closed. $BoredBlock1 is to the left. $Washer1 is to the right, with $Block2 and $Peg1 stacked on top of it.

Figure 7.5

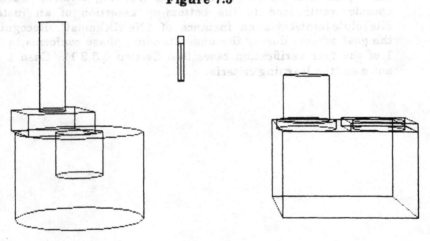

Third Alternate Initial State for Widget Assembly Problem

The robot gripper is located in the center of the picture with fingers closed. $Bored-Cylinder1 is to the left, with $Peg1 stacked on top of it. $Peg3 and $Washer2 are stacked (from left to right) on top of $Block1 on the right side of the workspace.

Figure 7.6

7.7. Observing Similar Problems After Learning

Once either version of $NewSchemaC is integrated into the schema library via the establishment of ::Suggestions and ::Plans pointers, it can be recognized bottom-up during the course of future observation processes. This has two important implications:

(1)   More complicated joints using an instance of $RevoluteJointA as a part of their structure can now be examined and are available for learning. An analogous situation arises in this episode based on the fact that both $CylindricalJointA0311 and $RigidJointA301 are recognized using previously acquired instances of $NewSchemaB and $NewSchemaA, respectively. Note that such joints might still have been analyzable on the basis of $CylindricalJoint and $RigidJoint, but the presence of $NewSchemaC reduces the computational burden which would have been placed on the verifier.

(2)   Another observation episode with a functionally similar goal when achieved in the same physical manner and with generally the same plan will no longer meet the learning criteria. Such an episode would lead to the bottom-up assertion of an instance $RevoluteJointA via an instance of $NewSchemaC. Recognizing the goal schema during the understanding phase conforms to Case 1 of the four verification cases (see Section 5.3.2.1). Case 1 does not meet the learning criteria.

Chapter 8
Summary And Future Work

The ARMS system was intended as an experiment in the application of explanation-based learning techniques to a real-world domain. As with any experiment, ARMS has raised many new issues that must yet be resolved. In this chapter we conclude our examination of the ARMS system with a discussion of its relation to other work, its extensibility, and directions for future research.

8.1. Relation to Other Work

Work in explanation-based learning is still relatively young, although it is possible to trace its roots back to STRIPS [25] and other systems of that era [64]. Current research in explanation-based systems exists at various stages of implementation. Among them are the GENESIS system [32], LP [27], LEX2 [23], MA [28], LEAP [65], Physics-101 [30], EGGS [66], CHEF [67], and the SOAR mapping of EBL [68]. Some work aimed at integrating EBL and SBL is also just beginning to appear (OCCAM [69], UNIMEM [70]).

In this section, we summarize five of these systems which, to varying degrees, can be related to the ARMS system. The first of the five, STRIPS, is perhaps the earliest and best known explanation-based system in existence. Due in part to this chronological attribute, it tends to be used as a standard for comparison with other EBL systems. The other four systems (MA, LEAP, ODYSSEUS, and PRODIGY) are all classified as explanation-based learning-apprentice systems and, as such, are probably the ARMS system's closest relatives.

8.1.1. STRIPS

The STRIPS system [25] is a problem-solving system that controls a robot moving about rooms connected by doors. The robot is capable of moving boxes about the rooms, opening doors as it goes. The problem solver incorporates a learning component that acquires generalized plans from previous problem solutions.

There are several major differences between STRIPS and ARMS. First of all, STRIPS is a closed-loop system that relies on its own weak-method problem solver as a source of examples for learning. Secondly, the plans acquired by STRIPS do not abstract temporal orderings, nor do they abstract the operators themselves. Every operator in the originally observed plan occurs in the generalized plan in precisely the same order. Generalization occurs only in what is allowed to fill the operator arguments.

While STRIPS was used to drive a real-world robot, this was due more to an engineering tour-de-force rather than any close relation between STRIPS and a real-world domain. The STRIPS domain is in fact little more than veneer applied to a theorem prover in order to facilitate communication of proof descriptions between humans. As such, there are two specific assumptions made in the STRIPS domain that severly restrict its applicability to real-world problems:

(1)   The *STRIPS assumption* [71] holds that any operator applied by the system changes the state of the world in a well-defined fashion: all effects are explicitly listed in the definition of the operator itself. This corresponds to the system having complete knowledge of the effects of its operators. This is an attractive assumption to make since it permits a system builder to reduce the system's planner to a theorem proving engine. It is not necessarily a reasonable assumption, since it requires the effects of every operator to be fully known *a priori*.

(2)   The *closed-world hypothesis* [72] holds that failing to prove the proposition P is sufficient reason to conclude NOT(P). This corresponds to the system having complete and perfect knowledge about the current state of the world. Another way of looking at the closed-world hypothesis is to consider two distinct dichotomies of facts about the world. The first dichotomy is the division between those facts which are true and those which are not true. The second dichotomy divides facts about the world into those which are known (or derivable from known facts) and those which are not known (or derivable). The closed-world assumption forces these two divisions to coincide: under this assumption, unknown facts which cannot be derived from known facts are assumed to be

untrue.[23]

The current ARMS system does not make the STRIPS assumption: the effects of its operators are not known *a priori*. Certain operator effects in the world are never noticed by the database mechanism, that fills only specific requests from the learning and performance elements.

When we consider the modeler to be a part of the ARMS system, any property of a world snapshot that cannot be validated by querying the modeler is considered not to be true. However, no generalization or any other sort of action is ever taken by ARMS on the basis of a *failure* to validate a relation. In this sense, ARMS does not make the closed-world assumption.

8.1.2. MA

MA (later changed to LA) [28] is a learning apprentice in the domain of mathematical natural deduction. This is an obvious target domain for learning-apprentice research due to the simplicity and completeness of the domain theory. MA constructs its own explanation as it observes the theorem proving behavior of its user. The MA theorem proving domain is a simple domain where making the STRIPS assumption is quite reasonable. While never really used as an apprentice system, MA served as a useful experimental tool in formalizing EBL techniques. Unlike ARMS, MA was never fully implemented.

An interesting side project stemming from MA is described in [29]. By reimplementing the *Logic Theorist* system [73] and augmenting it with EBL, empirical evidence of the effectiveness of EBL was provided.

8.1.3. LEAP

The LEAP system [65] is a learning apprentice in the domain of VLSI circuit design. The system is implemented on top of the VEXED [74] circuit-design editor, that is intended to provide a large user base for eventual acquisition of circuit-design capability. LEAP ignores the geometric aspects of VLSI layout.

---

[23] There are other, slightly different, statements of this hypothesis. The statement adopted here opens the possibility that attempting to prove *P* may never terminate. It is possible to weaken the notion of proof slightly by imposing resource limits to insure termination. A different version of the hypothesis holds that failure to find *P* directly in the database is sufficient to conclude NOT(*P*): no deduction is permitted or attempted. This is a far more restrictive statement, since it assumes every true assertion about the world must be directly stated in the database.

The circuit-design domain is a particularly appealing domain due to the existence of a good, albeit still naive, domain theory based on Boolean algebra. Note, however, that even a domain theory based on Boolean algebra is incomplete. For example, LEAP adopts a timing model that is only an approximation of the behavior of an actual circuit.

LEAP is highly interactive, and, as such, will often ask the user to provide help in constructing its analysis of the example. This would seem to be possibly obtrusive; an option carefully avoided in the ARMS implementation. As of this writing, the implementation of LEAP is incomplete.

8.1.4. ODYSSEUS

The ODYSSEUS learning-apprentice project [75] supplies an acquisition module for HERACLES. HERACLES is a domain-independent shell derived from the NEOMYCIN medical expert system [76]. As of this writing, ODYSSEUS is still being implemented.

ODYSSEUS uses a *difference-based* strategy to initiate learning. When the expert's behavior differs from that expected by the system, a dialogue subsystem queries the expert in order to construct an explanation for the difference. The system is interesting in that it is intended to operate in challenging domains (e.g., medical diagnosis) that lack a good domain theory.

The major difference between ARMS and ODYSSEUS lies in its explanation construction process. ODYSSEUS operates without a sound domain theory, and therefore falls back on more intrusive user-interaction in order to construct its explanation. This seems to be a case where an alternate explanation construction method is adopted due to the dictates of the domain.

8.1.5. PRODIGY

PRODIGY [77] is a learning-apprentice system operating in a pseudorobot domain. The PRODIGY world is modeled on that of BUILD [78], that provides for moving and stacking various sized blocks. PRODIGY uses EBL to compress the search space and improve the efficiency of problem solving. Like LEAP and ODYSSEUS (but unlike ARMS), PRODIGY is highly interactive. In fact, one of its goals is to support the study of human-computer interaction. If PRODIGY cannot build an explanation for a given example, it asks the teacher to provide one. As of this writing, PRODIGY is still under development.

By using simple STRIPS-like operators, the PRODIGY domain theory shares many of the advantages of the MA domain theory; a theorem prover provides the PRODIGY problem-solving engine. As such,

PRODIGY is fairly far removed from any possible real-world domain.

8.2. Extensibility of ARMS

An important consideration in describing a project such as ARMS is the system's *extensibility.* ARMS is meant to serve as a prototype, i.e., a working initial approximation of a real-world system. But the *significance* of a prototype is directly related to the *insignificance* of its limiting assumptions.

We divide extensibility problems into two different categories:

(1) *Representation problems* arise from the inherent difficulties involved in representing a continuous real-world domain in a discrete, symbolic fashion. This type of problem plagues any system that must reason about the physical world.

(2) *Learning problems* are those problems arising in the course of the acquisition, management, and application of problem-solving knowledge. This type of problem is more specific to machine learning, as opposed to AI in general.

In this section, we examine the representation problems expected in an extension of the ARMS system. In the next section we outline the learning problems as areas for future research in machine learning.

8.2.1. The Solid Modeler Problem

The first representation problem has to do with the representational power of the solid modeling system. A real-world application of ARMS must retain the modeler, if for no other reason than to serve as a tool in the application of the domain theory. Clearly, the current ARMS modeler is much too simplistic, given its small number of CSG primitives (two) and its restricted combination operators.

Many modeling systems exist that are, at least representationally speaking, far more powerful than the ARMS modeler [79-81]. These modelers allow for piece-to-piece variance, and permit the representation of a far more diverse set of pieces than the ARMS modeler. Incorporation of one of these modelers as part of the ARMS system would go a long way towards relieving the current representational constraints.

The major difficulty foreseen in using an extant solid modeler arises from the fact that these modelers were, for the most part, created to support computer graphics or CAD/CAM design. They place a heavy emphasis on rendering objects for visual display, rather than modeling objects as they interact in a physical sense. Some nontrivial extensions to support the modeling of physical object interactions would be necessary.

As an example of the type of capability that could be provided, recall that the current implementation stipulates a piece must have no pieces stacked on it before it is manipulated. A new improved implementation might permit moving a stack of pieces all at once. Even if the clear-top limitation were retained, it might be possible to manipulate entire assemblies at once, provided the new positions of related pieces can be determined through an analysis of the degrees of freedom that relate them. Note that this kind of reasoning will probably require the system to deal with some degree of uncertainty, at least in piece positioning after assembly manipulation.

8.2.2. Reasoning with Uncertainty

ARMS supports a single arm operating in a controlled domain. Some of the more interesting problems in robotics must consider cooperation between several robot arms, or between a robot arm and a human worker. The expected problems in a cooperative situation arise from the introduction of uncertainty in the world.

In the current system, it is safe to assume that the only changes occurring in the world are effected by a single agent, the robot arm. Consistency between the world and the internal representation can be guaranteed, since no independent changes are permitted in the world.

There are three ways of dealing with the introduction of uncertainty in the system:

(1) The *strong approach* advocates extending the simulation capabilities of the system to support the modeling of the effects of other agents, human intervention, and gravity. Such simulation tools would by necessity be domain-specific, presenting a tremendous programming challenge. In addition, the approach would impose strict limits on actions performed by outside agents. Since these actions must also be simulated internally, they must belong to the class of actions known *a priori*.

(2) The *weak approach* advocates the construction of powerful sensory systems that can provide enough information to keep the internal representation consistent with the real world. This approach represents in reality a spectrum of different approaches, ranging from no internal simulation coupled with perfect sensors to using naive process simulation coupled with verification-type sensors. This approach faces hard engineering problems in the construction of the sensory systems, and, in addition, must deal with the problem of credit assignment. By relying more on sensory systems

and less on internal simulation, the system must determine which agent effected which changes in the world.

(3) The *fault-tolerant approach* provides for reasoning without complete knowledge, using various methods for the retraction of mistaken assumptions and recovery from ambiguous situations. While this approach promises to result in the most robust system, much work remains to be done in this active research area [82-86].

8.2.3. The Operator/State Problem

The third representation problem arises from forcing the real world to conform to an operator/state representational paradigm. The ARMS system provides no facility for acquiring new state descriptors. In other words, certain relations (e.g., stacking, aligning) are built into the system and cannot be augmented.[24]

No system can claim to solve all problems. The acquisition of state descriptors is a task best left, perhaps, to similarity-based methods. In particular, *constructive induction* [87] can be used to transform a base feature set directly derived from physical aspects of the problem into more operational higher-level feature sets.

8.2.4. The Temporal Reasoning Problem

The temporal model used by the current implementation of ARMS is quite simplistic. No attempt is made to describe temporal interactions between events instigated by different agents, uncertainty in temporal information, or even that operators occur over time rather than instantaneously. Temporal modeling remains an important unresolved issue for ARMS, as well as for AI in general [88-90].

In a sense, the temporal reasoning problem is all about trying to find a simple, yet workable, method of representing the common-sense world. The most naive approach (e.g., instantaneous operations resulting in states that persist) may be sufficient for some simple domains. By assuming that only one action may occur at a time and that states persist unchanged through time, it is quite possible to model, for example, a game of chess.

A domain that permits multiple agents to act concurrently and asynchronously is far more difficult to model. When one also considers that real-world states do not often persist unchanged (consider a barrel

---

[24] An exception is the acquisition of new physical joint schemata, which are subtypes of existing abstract joint schemata. Physical joint schemata are, in fact, special types of state schemata. See Section 5.3.2.1.2.

full of water with a tiny hole at the bottom) it is clear that a more complex temporal reasoning system is required.

8.3. Future Research Directions

In this section, we discuss nine machine-learning issues arising from our experience with ARMS. Progress on these issues is necessary for the future development of explanation-based systems, and, in particular, learning-apprentice systems.

8.3.1. Frame Selection Problem

The crucial step in any application of EBL techniques is the construction of the explanation. The ARMS system constructs this explanation unobtrusively through the use of an understanding element. The use of an understanding element makes the system vulnerable to the combinatorial explosion inherent in the schema-selection problem.

The ARMS system posits a nonpredictive framework for schema selection as a potentially less explosive alternative to the predictive methods of natural language systems. This technique takes a wait-and-see approach to the schema-selection problem, relying on the assumption that most of the contexts hypothesized by a predictive understander would eventually be discarded.

Future work should build on this nonpredictive framework. In particular, what domain traits permit a system to take advantage of the efficiency aspects of nonpredictive understanding? Do other schema-selection methodologies take similar advantage of these domain traits? Is there some taxonomy of schema-selection methods which can be used to guide selection of a mechanism for use in a particular implementation?

8.3.2. Other Explanation Construction Methods

The unobtrusive character of the ARMS learning-apprentice system follows from the bottom-up schema-activation causal model construction philosophy embodied in the ARMS understanding element. But schema activation is not the only method for constructing explanations: the use of *analogy*, *explanation modification*, and *reminding* may also be practical solutions to the explanation construction problem. Certainly some attention should be directed towards using alternative explanation construction methods when schema activation fails to provide an adequate explanation.

8.3.3. When and What to Learn

A learning apprentice in regular use by an expert will be presented with an overwhelming number of learning opportunities. Clearly, not all of these observed episodes are worth learning from. This issue affects the efficiency of both the schema-activation mechanism (and thus future learning episodes) and the planning subsystem (and thus the system's problem-solving performance). Learning criteria can be used to select those episodes that should produce new schemata.

Current learning-apprentice systems (ARMS is no exception) generally avoid this problem by learning whenever an observed episode presents a new situation. In other words, if the understander can construct the explanation without relying on the domain theory to analyze the causal model, then the episode is not interesting from a learning perspective. This is a safe learning criterion, in the sense that there is no risk of missing a learnable schema. Unfortunately, this criterion is not practical in everyday applications, due to the resulting large volume of new schemata.

In addition to learning criteria, it is possible to install retention criteria to further reduce the number of new schemata retained. Retention criteria are used after generalization to determine whether a new schema is worth saving. ARMS, like other extant learning apprentices, retains every schema it produces.

Two of the unresolved questions that are raised by this implementation arise from these two criteria. While use of learning and retention criteria seems to be indicated, a careful examination of what these criteria should look like is clearly indicated. The use of particular learning or retention criteria implies an obvious efficiency vs. effectiveness trade-off. What other effects are likely to result from the application of different criteria?

8.3.4. When and What to Forget

Learning and retention criteria represent a first approximation to the problem of managing the changing knowledge base of a learning apprentice. These criteria are monotonic in the sense that they can only provide for additions to the knowledge base.

A critical issue for real-world, learning-apprentice systems is whether old entries in the knowledge base can be replaced in time by new, presumably more useful, entries. Just as with computer page-replacement algorithms, a finite resource (such as memory) is managed in order to improve the effectiveness of the system.

Such replacement criteria can also be expected to have efficiency vs. effectiveness effects on a learning-apprentice system. What should these criteria look like? Should correlational considerations enter into the replacement criteria? Is a schema's usefulness measurable in some fashion other than a simple usage count? Can a schema's usefulness be predicted on the basis of its structure or similarity to other schemata in the library? Perhaps an indication of expected usefulness can be derived from the domain theory. All of these issues are yet to be investigated, much less resolved.

8.3.5. Refining Existing Knowledge

Forgetting schemata is a viable means to limit the growth of the schema library in order to avoid adverse performance effects. Another approach might be to modify or extend existing schemata in order to increase their applicability.

Suppose a system is presented with a new problem-solving episode that is almost, but not quite, explained by an existing schema. Should the system modify the existing schema to cover the new example, or generate an entirely new schema? This is an important issue when one considers that a new schema may compete or otherwise interact with extant schemata in an unpredictable manner.

Perhaps the easiest form of schema refinement would involve restricting application conditions when presented with a planning failure. In other words, when a schema that should be applicable fails to achieve its goal, its application conditions could be modified to avoid repeated failure.

Must schema refinement be failure-driven? A uniquely failure-driven refinement strategy would seem to indicate that only new restrictions on existing schemata can be introduced by this process. Perhaps given a measure of *almost explained* it is possible to refine existing schemata to cover more rather than fewer instances.

8.3.6. Learning Control Knowledge

An interesting issue arising from work in many areas of machine learning, including learning-apprentice systems, is the acquisition of control knowledge. Consider the case of a VLSI learning apprentice observing the highly regular layout of an eight-bit shift register. The system should acquire a schema that covers not only the eight-bit case, but the arbitrary n-bit case.

There has been some preliminary work on learning iterative control structures [91, 92]. Generally this work has been applied only to toy examples in micro-world domains.

The use of iterative control structures also affects the size of the knowledge base; a system with separate schemata for four-bit, eight-bit, and sixteen-bit shift registers will not perform as well as a system with a single n-bit shift register schema.

8.3.7. Extending Imperfect Domain Theories

The application of EBL techniques relies on the use of a domain theory. As in the ARMS implementation, these domain theories are often naive theories of how the world works. The question of what happens to the system when the domain theory breaks down needs to be addressed if learning apprentice systems are to be operated in such naive domain theory situations.

In [4], Mitchell *et al.* present three different cases of the imperfect domain theory problem:

(1) The *incomplete theory problem* occurs when the domain theory is not complete enough to explain the observed input. In this case, Mitchell *et al.* suggest constructing the most plausible explanation and continuing with the learning process.

(2) The *intractable theory problem* occurs when constructing an explanation is too computationally expensive using the current domain theory. Humans generally construct less detailed, approximative theories for use in this situation.

(3) The *inconsistent theory problem* occurs when the domain theory permits construction of contradictory explanations for an observed input. Of the three theory problems, this is the only one that has attracted research attention so far [22, 93].

One would hope the system's learning performance would degrade gracefully as the domain theory breaks down. An even better alternative would be for the system to extend its domain theory automatically. Possible strategies include devising experiments to make inconsistent theories unambiguous, creating more abstract theories to deal with intractable theories, and extending incomplete theories through incorporation of SBL techniques.

8.3.8. Execution Monitoring and Plan Revision

A popular area of research in both robot planning [94-96] and planning in general [97, 98] has been the construction and study of systems that monitor the performance of the planner and attempt to recover from plan failures. This is normally an expensive proposition, since any replanning implies, at least for robot-planning systems, more search. Learning-apprentice systems tend to do very little search in planning. If the system cannot plan within some computational resource limit, it simply gives up and defers to the human expert.

This is not meant to imply, however, that there is no place for execution monitoring and plan revision. While computationally expensive, this capability may be just the ticket for dealing with some aspect of uncertainty. Imagine a scenario where it is simply too expensive to ascertain the validity of all of the application conditions for a given operator schema. If the operator is relevant and is *probably* applicable, it may be easier to attempt to apply the operator and subsequently recover from any failures due to incomplete world information.

8.3.9. Dealing with Multiple Plans

Often the planning system will have more than one schema available for achieving the same goal state. In this case, normally one plan is to be preferred over the other alternatives, usually on the basis of predicted execution expense or some other metric.

We note that one way of getting multiple plans for the same goal is to generalize more than once from the same example, using different values for the generality/operationality flag. With the ARMS system, this would produce two different new schemata from the same example. Of the two new schemata acquired, application of the more operational one should always be preferred over application of the more general one.

If no ordering is known for a given set of plans, it should be possible for the system to acquire an ordering by examining the performance of its planner. Learning such orderings seems well suited for the application of similarity-based learning techniques. Note that this kind of learning would occur incrementally under the auspices of the performance element, rather than the learning element.

8.4. Conclusions

The construction of smart machines may well be mankind's next evolutionary step. Proponents of AI maintain that the advent of truly intelligent machines is imminent, while critics scoff at silicon dreamers. Books are written, positions are taken, and AI-bashing (or AI-booster) reputations are made.

The AI pragmatist is more than a little perplexed at the brouhaha surrounding the field. The pragmatist adopts an *if it quacks like a duck it must be a duck* definition of AI. To the pragmatist, progress towards any eventual man-made intelligent entity consists of a series of plodding efforts, each making its own contribution, however tiny, to our collective understanding of what makes a machine *smart*. Each effort quacks just a bit louder than the last.

The ARMS project is only a first step. As any first step, it may appear to be small and tentative. But it serves a very important purpose: it serves to demonstrate the feasibility of explanation-based, learning-apprentice systems operating in realistic problem-solving domains. The development of learning-apprentice systems has the potential of providing AI with its next success. There are hundreds of possible applications: CAD/CAM design, VLSI layout, investment banking strategies, automatic flight control, and robot programming, just to name a few.

And so the pragmatist slogs on in the AI trenches, content with slow, but steady, progress on that inexorable march towards usable and helpful smart computer programs aimed at improving man's lot in life.

Appendix A
Solid Modeling Systems

Work in other areas of computer science, especially computer graphics, provides us with a rich heritage in solid modeling [99,100]. These systems deal with far more demanding domains, where pieces may have curved surfaces and complex shapes in general. Most were designed for CAD/CAM use, and therefore place a heavy emphasis on the representation of the solid for eventual rendering on a computer graphics terminal. Solid modeling systems have found use in several applications, such as static interference analysis, finite-element meshing, automatic verification of machine tool numerical control programs, and robot task simulation.

Previous work in solid modeling can be roughly partitioned into two different representational camps: *boundary representations* (BRep), as typified by EUCLID and ROMULUS [81,101,102]; and *constructive solid geometries* (CSG), as exemplified by PADL or GMSOLID [79,80,103]. The difference lies in the internal representation used for the solid.[25]

BRep systems represent the solid as a set of faces specified by surface equations and bounding edges. These representations prove particularly popular due to the importance of computer graphics in most applications. From BReps it is relatively easy to construct displays with faces shaded and hidden lines removed. On the other hand, BReps are memory-intensive, and there is no easy way to guarantee that the BReps constructed actually correspond to physically valid solids.

---

[25] Other representational strategies, such as *sweep methods, cell decompositions*, and *octree methods* are also used but are less common for this particular type of application. For a review of these and other representational schemes see [104].

CSG systems represent the solid as various set operations on primitive solids. Generally the primitive set includes blocks, cylinders, spheres, etc. The set operations usually include the Boolean operations union, difference and intersection. By specifying a set of instances of the primitives, their dimensions and relative positions, and an ordered set of operations on this primitive set, one can construct arbitrarily complex solids. Such representations are not only concise, but also automatically insure the physical validity of the constructed solid.

Unfortunately, CSG representations are not well suited for many applications: for example, in computer graphics, the image rendered on the screen depicts the surfaces and not the volume of the object. To circumvent this problem, *hybrid modeling systems* rely on a mix of both representational strategies, usually by automatically converting CSG representations to BReps for graphic output. Such conversion algorithms are well known [105-107], although they are usually computationally expensive on standard hardware.

Appendix B
Schema Semantics

A *schema* is a chunked knowledge structure that represents the system's generalized knowledge about a particular concept or topic. While many systems have relied on such a chunked representation for the knowledge they manipulate, no consensus has emerged with regard to the structure of these chunks. In this appendix, we outline the schema terminology used in describing the ARMS schema system.

A schema represents abstract knowledge, e.g., it describes a concept that may have many different *instantiations*. A *schema instance* represents a particular, fully specified, instance of a concept. The process of creating a schema instance from a given schema is called the *instantiation process*. During this process, all ambiguity which is implicit in the schema is resolved in the schema instance. In short, a schema gives a framework for a (possibly very large) set of schema instances.

A schema consists of a *name* and a set of *slots*. The value of a slot is called its *filler*. When a schema is defined, every slot filler is given a *default value* which may or may not be overridden during the instantiation process. A slot filler may represent another schema, another schema instance, a list of schemata or schema instances, a descriptor, a number, or any other data structure. We adopt the notational convention that the name of a schema is always prefaced with the special "$" character (e.g., $Schema) and the name of a schema instance always ends with a number (e.g., $Schema122).

A *schema template* is a device by which one abstract schema can refer to a second abstract schema. A template consists of a *header* and a *binding equivalence list*. The header indicates the name of the second schema. The binding equivalence list gives a partial mapping from the first schema's slot fillers to the second schema's slot fillers. For example, consider a schema $A with a slot X. Suppose that $A must establish a one-to-one mapping between all of its instances with instances of the schema $B. Further suppose that this relationship should specify that the filler of slot Y in each instance of $B should be equal to the filler of slot X in the corresponding instance of $A. By using the schema template:

   ($B (Y X))

to refer to schema $B from within schema $A, it is possible for future instances $Ai of $A to identify (possibly as yet non-existent) instances $Bj of $B. This particular template indicates that, given an instance $A1 of $A, the object of the relation is an instance of the schema $B whose Y slot has the same filler as the X slot of $A1. Thus, the template serves as a way to describe a mapping between instances of two different schemata.

Appendix C
A Simpler Example

In this appendix, we will describe another example which is quite a bit simpler than the $RevoluteJoint of Chapters 2 and 7. This episode is, despite its simplicity, interesting because the schema it acquires is used in the understanding phase of the $RevoluteJoint example. This demonstrates that a schema acquired by the system is useful not only for planning, but also for understanding more complicated tasks. In fact, without the schema acquired here, the widget assembly discussed in Chapter 2 would not have been understood; thus, no learning could have taken place.[26]

The example consists of inserting a peg into a hole where the shaft of the peg and the hole have the same diameter. This yields a tight friction fit that results in a rigid connection, or rigid joint, between the two pieces.

There are two factors contributing to the simplicity of this example:

(1) A $RigidJoint is inherently simple, since it has no degrees of freedom.

(2) The verification step is trivial, since the physical implementation joint schema for this example, $RigidJointA, is already present in the system (Case 2 of Section 5.3.2.1).

---

[26] This example yields an operator schema for achieving $RigidJointA, In a similar fashion, yet another example yields an operator schema for achieving $CylindricalJointA. The system relies on both of these schemata in order to understand, and therefore learn from, the widget example of Chapter 2.

C.1. Describing the Initial State

The initial state is shown in Figure C.1. $BoredBlock1 is to the right, with its hole already pointing upwards. $Peg1 is off to the left, and the arm (fingers closed) is in its nest position. The goal specification is given as a partially instantiated abstract joint schema:

$RigidJoint [Piece1 = $Peg1, Piece2 = $BoredBlock1].

There are no other pieces in the workspace.

C.2. Attempting to Solve the Problem

The performance element undertakes the design phase in order to produce a fully instantiated physical joint schema from the partially instantiated abstract joint schema derived from the goal specification. From the abstract joint schema we index those physical joint schemata that represent physical realizations of the mechanical behavior given by the abstract joint schema.

From the abstract joint schema $RigidJoint, the system indexes two alternative physical realizations, given by $RigidJointA and $RigidJointB. In fact, $RigidJointA and $RigidJointB differ from each other only in which piece is identified as Piece1 and which piece is identified as Piece2. The realization procedure returns two tokens, one of

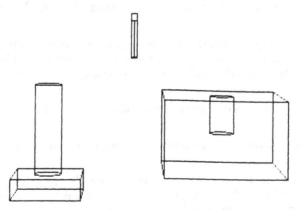

Initial State

The robot arm gripper is located in the center of the picture with its fingers closed and pointing downwards. $Peg1 is to the left and $BoredBlock1 is to the right.

Figure C.1

each type, with fillers from $RigidJoint mapped over to fill slots on the two tokens.

The realization process is now applied to the physical joint schema tokens produced above. Constraints attached to $RigidJointB cause realization of that token to fail. Realization of the $RigidJointA token terminates successfully, returning a single fully instantiated token $RigidJointA0012.

The substantiator set of $RigidJointA0012 contains the single state schema representing an inserted state. However, $RigidJointA (*ergo* also $RigidJointA0012) has no entries on its ::Plans type slot. Hence while the design phase terminates successfully, and a fully instantiated physical joint schema is produced, the system cannot generate a plan for achieving the physically realized goal. The planning phase terminates unsuccessfully, and the performance element aborts.

C.3. Observing the Expert's Plan

Having failed to generate a solution to the problem, control passes to the learning element which asks the expert to direct the robot arm through a solution of the problem. As the expert guides the arm, the causal model of the expert's problem-solving behavior is constructed using the schema-activation mechanism of Section 5.3.1.3.3.

C.4. Verifying the Solution

When the expert is finished, and the causal model is complete, the generalizer must verify that the goal was achieved. This particular example is an easy (Case 2) verification problem, since the abstract joint schema $RigidJoint indexes two known physical joint schemata $RigidJointA and $RigidJointB.

The verifier begins issuing requests to the database for valid instances of each known physical joint schema (e.g., $RigidJointA and $RigidJointB) corresponding to $RigidJoint. These requests are partially instantiated, since some fillers map over from the partially specified abstract joint schema given as the goal specification. As soon as the database returns a valid instance ($RigidJointA0012 in this case), the verification process terminates successfully.

C.5. Generalizing the Solution

An explanation is extracted from the causal model by following pointers from the substantiators of $RigidJointA0012. The substantiators constitute the top-level subgoal set. In this example, the only substantiator is $Inserted0423, representing the insertion of $Peg1 into $BoredBlock1.[27]

The precondition promotion set prepends the state $Braced0217 to the top-level subgoal set. $Braced0217 is an explicitly achieved precondition of $Insert0422, the operator schema responsible for the achievement of $Inserted0423.

The slot promotion process adds two new slots to the new schema. One slot represents the hole through which the insertion occurs, while the other slot represents the depth of that hole. These slots are added in order to permit mapping their values back and forth among the subgoals and body of the new schema.

The body of the new schema is determined by taking the last subgoal of the subgoal set (e.g., $Inserted0423) and making a template from the operator that was observed achieving it. In this example, the new schema's body is produced from $Insert0422. This leaves the template of $Braced0217 as the only remaining subgoal.

The new operator schema, $NewSchemaA, acquired in this example is shown in Figure C.2. It basically states:

> In order to achieve that physical incarnation of $RigidJoint known as $RigidJointA, it is sufficient to achieve an instance of $BracedHole for Piece1 of the joint and then execute an $Insert of Piece2 into Piece1.

Pointers are established to the new schema from $Insert (a ::Suggestions pointer) and from $RigidJointA (a ::Plans pointer).

C.6. Solving the Same Problem After Learning

If we present the system with the same problem after schema acquisition, the design phase will terminate successfully as before. A single token $RigidJointA0639 (analogous to our earlier $RigidJointA0012) is returned. This time, however, the plan phase is allowed to continue, as the ::Plans type slot of $RigidJointA contains a pointer to $NewSchemaA.

An instance $NewSchemaA0711 of $NewSchemaA is created, and the planner checks for conformity of the preconditions of the new schema. Since $NewSchemaA has no preconditions, the planner begins to plan for achieving the subgoals of $NewSchemaA0711.

---

[27] The cardinality of the substantiator set at this point makes the generality/operationality question moot: the generalizer will produce the same schema regardless of the mode it is operating in. Recall that the more operational schema relies on the examination of shared substructure between the elements of the top-level subgoal set (Section 5.3.2.3). Clearly, if there is only one member of the set there can be no shared substructure.

```
((Supers OperatorSchema)
 (TypeSlots
  (Goals (($RigidJointA  (Piece1 Piece1)
                         (Piece2 Piece2)
                         (Primitive1 Primitive1)
                         (Primitive2 Primitive2))))
  (SubGoals ((($BracedHole  (Piece Piece2)
                            (Primitive Primitive2)
                            (Hole NewSlot1)
                            (Depth NewSlot2)))))
  (Body ($Insert (Piece1 Piece1)
                 (Primitive1 Primitive1)
                 (Piece2 Piece2)
                 (Primitive2 Primitive2)
                 (Hole NewSlot1)
                 (Depth NewSlot2))))
 (TokenSlots
  (Piece1 NIL          doc (* From goalSchema))
  (Piece2 NIL          doc (* From goalSchema))
  (Primitive1 NIL      doc (* From goalSchema))
  (Primitive2 NIL      doc (* From goalSchema))
  (NewSlot1 NIL        doc (* Promoted slot))
  (NewSlot2 NIL        doc (* Promoted slot))))

                    $NewSchemaA
```

Figure C.2

The subgoal $Braced0750 is achieved successfully by a recursive application of the plan step. The body of $NewSchemaA0711 is now instantiated, and an application of the execution step to $Insert0938 completes the example.

C.7. Solving Similar Problems After Learning

The procedure outlined in the previous section works equally well for other initial starting positions of the same pieces. In addition, it is capable of planning and executing solutions for other examples that achieve instances of $RigidJointA using different pieces.

Two other functionally similar examples (initial states shown in Figures C.3 and C.4) were given to the ARMS system. Both of these problems can be solved by applying instances of $NewSchemaA.

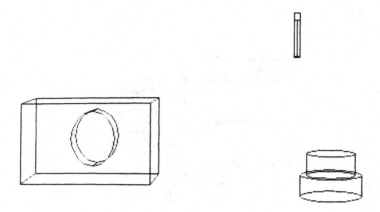

Alternate Rigid Joint Problem

The robot arm gripper is located in the center of the picture with its fingers closed and pointing downwards. $Peg2 is to the right, and $BoredBlock2 is on its side to the left.

Figure C.3

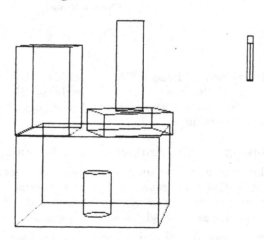

Alternate Rigid Joint Problem

The robot arm gripper is located in the center of the picture with its fingers closed and pointing downwards. $BoredBlock1 is inverted with $Block2 and $Peg1 stacked on top.

Figure C.4

C.8. Observing Similar Problems After Learning

As a final note, consider what would happen if another observation episode realizes an instance of $RigidJointA in the same manner. Once $NewSchemaA is added to the schema library and properly integrated via ::Plans and ::Suggestions pointers, it can also be used in understanding future examples.

The verification process would now find the instantiated version of the physical joint schema $RigidJointA already extant in the database. This situation corresponds to Case 1 of Section 5.3.2.1, which fails to meet the learning criteria. The learning element would terminate, and no new schema would be added to the schema library.

Appendix D
A More Complex Example

In this appendix, we examine another session with ARMS. This example constructs a more complicated assembly called a $SlidingRevoluteJoint. The system will again be acquiring a new physical joint schema, $SlidingRevoluteJointA, to describe this particular physical instantiation of the functionality described by $SlidingRevoluteJoint.

A $SlidingRevoluteJoint has two degrees of freedom, one prismatic and one revolute, which are orthogonal to each another. It is similar to a $CylindricalJoint, except that a $CylindricalJoint's degrees of freedom are along the same axes.

The general strategy for achieving this mechanical behavior is to construct a $TriplePrismaticJoint (three prismatic degrees of freedom) and a $RevoluteJoint (one revolute degree of freedom). The $TriplePrismaticJoint must somehow lose two of its prismatic degrees of freedom, leaving only a single prismatic degree of freedom to the $SlidingRevoluteJoint.

The physical realization of this mechanism consists of an elongated collar ($Box1) sliding along a tab protruding from a large frame piece ($Frame1). The collar, when inserted over the tab, constitute an instance of $TriplePrismaticJointB. The frame also has a cylindrical hole at the top, upon which we build an instance of $RevoluteJointA (using $Washer3 and $Peg4 along with $Frame1). The complexity of this example is due to the following reasons:

(1) The particular physical instantiation presented requires four pieces to construct the mechanism.

(2) The assembly of the mechanism results in the recognition of four physical joint schemata: a $RevoluteJointA (including its subjoints

$CylindricalJointA and $RigidJointA) via $NewSchemaC of Chapter 2, and a $TriplePrismaticJointB via $NewSchemaD (acquired separately).

(3)   Like the $RevoluteJoint example of Chapter 2, this example collects its constituent degrees of freedom from its constituent subjoints. Unlike the $RevoluteJoint, however, the degrees of freedom are assembled from more than one subjoint, requiring constraints between degrees of freedom to span subjoint boundaries.

(4)   The construction of the $SlidingRevoluteJoint occurs incrementally over time: unlike the example of Chapter 2 there is no single motion that achieves the mechanism specified.

(5)   Finally, this example addresses the difficult problem of interacting degrees of freedom. Since the constituent degrees of freedom are not all from the same subjoint, the analysis of the mechanism must address the dynamic nature of the constituent subjoints. While the solution adopted is, in fact, quite naive and is not advanced as a general solution, it is a first step towards extending the ARMS domain theory to handle dynamic joint interactions.

D.1. Describing the Initial State

The initial state is shown in Figure D.1. $Frame1 is in the center of the picture, with $Box1 off to the left, $Peg4 to the right, and $Washer3 in the foreground. The goal specification is again given as a partially instantiated abstract joint schema:

$SlidingRevoluteJoint [Piece1 = $Washer3, Piece2 = $Box1].

There are no other pieces in the workspace.

D.2. Attempting to Solve the Problem

The performance element undertakes the design phase in order to produce a fully instantiated physical joint schema from the partially instantiated abstract joint schema derived from the goal specification. From the abstract joint schema we index those physical joint schemata which represent physical realizations of the mechanical behavior given by the abstract joint schema.

From the abstract joint schema $SlidingRevoluteJoint, however, the system can index no physical joint schemata. As in the example from Chapter 2, failure is immediate and the performance element aborts.

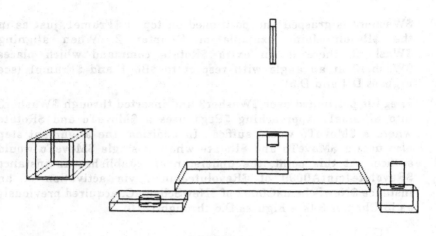

Initial State

The robot arm gripper is located in the center of the picture with its fingers closed and pointing downwards. $Frame1 is in the center of the workspace, with $Peg4 in the right foreground. $Washer3 is to the left, with $Box1 in the left background.

Figure D.1

D.3. Observing the Expert's Plan

Having failed to generate a solution to the problem, control passes to the learning element which asks the expert to direct the robot arm through a solution of the problem. As the expert guides the arm, the causal model of the expert's problem-solving behavior is constructed using the schema-activation mechanism of Section 5.3.1.3.3.

The expert's plan contains a total of 24 primitive arm commands, divided roughly as follows:

(1) $Box1 is grasped and positioned above $Frame1 aligned with the tab. When grasping $Box1, the expert inserts a redundant $Rotate command in order to grasp the piece with a narrower grip (see Figures D.2 and D.3).

(2) $Box1 is lowered over $Frame1, effecting the insertion of the tab through the holes in $Box1. We term this process *exsertion*, in order to distinguish it from insertion: here the evacuated piece is manipulated, while in a normal insertion the solid piece is manipulated. At this point, $TriplePrismaticJointB0076 is recognized via activation of an instance $NewSchemaD0073 of the previously learned $NewSchemaD (see Figure D.4).

(3) $Washer3 is grasped and positioned on top of $Frame1, just as in the $RevoluteJoint example of Chapter 2. When aligning $Washer3, there is an extra $Rotate command which places $Washer3 at an angle with respect to $Box1 and $Frame1 (see Figures D.4 and D.5).

(4) $Peg4 is positioned over $Washer3 and inserted through $Washer3 into $Frame1. Approaching $Peg4 uses a $MoveTo and $Rotate where a $MoveTo would suffice. In addition, the alignment step also uses a $MoveTo and $Rotate where a single $MoveTo would suffice. At this point, the understander establishes an instance $RevoluteJointA0099 of $RevoluteJointA via activation of an instance $NewSchemaC0092 of $NewSchemaC, acquired previously as in Chapter 8 (see Figures D.6 through D.10).

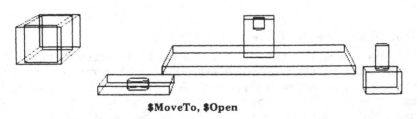

$MoveTo, $Open

The gripper is positioned over $Box1 with a $MoveTo command. The gripper fingers are then opened to their maximum aperture with an $Open command.

Figure D.2

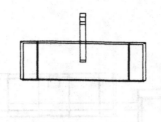

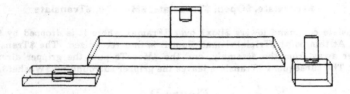

$Rotate, $Translate, $Close, $MoveTo

The gripper is twisted 90 degrees about the vertical axis with a $Rotate, and then lowered about $Box1 with a $Translate. The $Close command achieves a grasping of $Box1, and the $MoveTo positions $Box1 over $Frame1.

Figure D.3

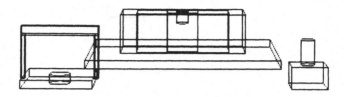

$Translate, $Open, $Translate, $MoveTo, $Translate

The $Translate command lowers $Box1 over $Frame1 where it is dropped by the $Open command. At this point $TriplePrismaticJointB is first recognized. The $Translate backs the gripper away from the assembly, and the $MoveTo puts the gripper directly above $Washer3. The subsequent $Translate leaves the gripper surrounding $Washer3.

Figure D.4

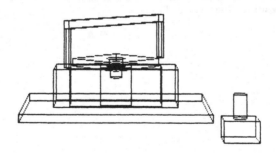

$Close, $MoveTo, $Rotate, $Translate, $Open

The $Close command achieves a grasping of $Washer3, while the $MoveTo positions it over the assembly under construction. A $Rotate twists $Washer3 90 degrees about the vertical axis before the $Translate lowers it onto $Frame1. The $Open drops $Washer.

Figure D.5

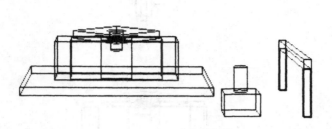

$Translate, $MoveTo

The $Translate backs the gripper up away from $Washer3, and the subsequent $MoveTo leaves the gripper near $Peg4.

Figure D.6

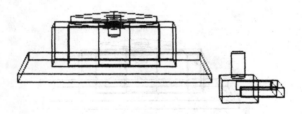

$Rotate, $Translate, $Close

The $Rotate command brings the gripper down so it faces $Peg4, while the $Translate surrounds $Peg4 with the gripper fingers. The $Close command grasps $Peg4.

Figure D.7

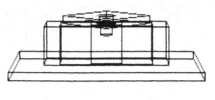

$MoveTo

The $MoveTo positions $Peg4 over the $Frame1/$Box1/$Washer3 assembly.

Figure D.8

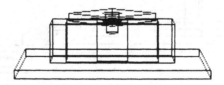

$Rotate

The $Rotate swings $Peg4 down so that it is aligned with the hole in $Washer3.

Figure D.9

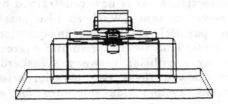

$Translate

The $Translate achieves an instance of $RevoluteJointA (acquired from the example of Chapter 2) between $Washer3 and $Frame1 via $Peg4.

Figure D.10

D.4. Verifying the Solution

Verification of the solution is an example of Case 3 verification described in Section 5.3.2.1. The verifier produces a new physical joint schema, $SlidingRevolutejointA, which describes this physical instantiation of the mechanism.

The verifier begins by searching for an open kinematic chain linking the two end pieces specified in the abstract joint schema $SlidingRevoluteJoint (the goal specification). The known joint schemata recognized by the system during the understanding phase are

   $TriplePrismaticJointB0076 ($Box1, $Frame1)
   $RevoluteJointA0099 ($Washer3, $Frame1)
      $CylindricalJointA0096 ($Washer3, $Peg4)
      $RigidJointA0094 ($Peg4, $Frame1)

At first it appears that there are two kinematic chains linking $Box1 and $Washer3. On closer examination, however, it is clear that since $CylindricalJointA0096 and $RigidJointA0094 taken together constitute $RevoluteJointA0099, there is really only a single kinematic chain.

The verifier collects copies of the degrees of freedom along the chain and attempts to recompute any soft bounds on these degrees of freedom. One of the prismatic degrees of freedom from $TriplePrismaticJointB0076 is already below the system-wide degree of freedom tolerance due to the dimensional constraints between $Box1 and $Frame1.

The prismatic degree of freedom from $TriplePrismaticJointB0076 (along the $Box1 insertion axis) is now constrained by a collision with $Washer3. Note, however, that $Washer3 also possesses a prismatic degree of freedom, parallel to the one in question, obtained from $CylindricalJointA0096. This second prismatic degree of freedom is in turn newly limited by a collision between $Washer3 and $Peg4. The cumulative motion allowed these two parallel prismatic degrees of freedom is below the system-wide tolerance for active degrees of freedom, thus they both cancel.

The remaining prismatic degree of freedom from $TriplePrismaticJointB0076 retains unchanged its two hard bounds resulting from collisions with $Frame1 at each end of $Box1's travel. Together with the revolute degree of freedom from $CylindricalJointA0096, that also remains unchanged, these constitute the degree of freedom set for the $SlidingRevoluteJoint.

The new schema $SlidingRevoluteJointA is constructed, indexed by $SlidingRevoluteJoint, to represent this particular physical realization of joint function. Slots are created on $SlidingRevoluteJointA to permit mapping of fillers across the substantiator set, and constraints are added which reflect only those physical interrelations (e.g., shape and dimension relations) between the fillers that were crucial to the cancellation of the prismatic degree of freedom. An instance of the new schema, $SlidingRevoluteJointA0111, is created to represent the achieved goal state, and the verification process terminates successfully.

D.5. Generalizing the Solution

The top-level subgoal set of this episode consists of the substantiators of $SlidingRevoluteJointA0111, i.e., $TriplePrismaticJointB0076, $CylindricalJointA0096 and $RigidJointA0094. From this subgoal set, the generalizer constructs a new operator schema to achieve the goal $SlidingRevoluteJointA, the newly added abstract schema corresponding to the current goal $SlidingRevoluteJointA0111.

The first step is to analyze any dependencies between these top-level subgoals in order to produce a partial ordering on the subgoal set. It is clear that $RigidJointA0094 imposes constraints on $CylindricalJointA0096, which in turn constraints $TriplePrismaticJointB. Hence, $TriplePrismaticJointB must be achieved before $CylindricalJointA0096, which in turn must be achieved before $RigidJointA0094.

At this point, the ARMS generalizer is capable of producing two different new operator schemata, depending on the value assigned to the current episode's generality/operationality trade-off flag (Section 5.3.2.3). This parameter reflects the level of representation chosen for the new schema: a more general new schema carries a higher price in planning, while a more operational new schema is applicable in fewer situations.

D.5.1. A More General New Schema

If we chose to produce the most general schema possible, the generalizer does not descend below the top-level subgoal set. In essence, the top-level subgoal set becomes the explanation for the observed episode.

Preconditions are collected from the top-level subgoal set members. The body of the new schema becomes the abstraction of $RigidJointA0094's achieving operator $NewSchemaA0093. The remaining subgoals becomes the new schema's subgoal set.

Slots are added to permit mapping fillers between the subgoal, body, and preconditions of the new schema. New slots are used to represent surfaces of InterimPiece1, InterimPiece2, and various important dimensions (e.g., length of the shaft, depth of the hole).

The new schema acquired is the most general representation of how this joint was achieved (see Figures D.11a and D.11b). It essentially states:

> To achieve an instance $SlidingRevoluteJointA, achieve an instance of $TriplePrismaticJointB between Piece1 of the joint and another piece, InterimPiece1. Next achieve a $CylindricalJointA between Piece2 of the joint and another piece, InterimPiece2. Finally, achieve an instance of $RigidJointA between InterimPiece1 and InterimPiece2 using the $NewSchemaA operator.

D.5.2. A More Operational New Schema

By resetting the generality/operationality trade-off flag, we can examine the more operational new schema produced by generalizer for this example. Recall from Section 5.3.2.3 that the more operational new schema is produced by descending the explanation to the point where the subgoal set can be expressed with no shared substructure.

Preconditions are collected from the members of the new subgoal set. The last element of the set is used to determine the body of the new schema. The remaining subgoals become the subgoals of the new schema.

```
((Supers OperatorSchema)
 (TypeSlots
  (Goals (($SlidingRevoluteJointA  (Piece1 Piece1)
                                   (Piece2 Piece2)
                                   (Primitive1 Primitive1)
                                   (Primitive2 Primitive2)
                                   (Orientation1 Orientation1)
                                   (Orientation2 Orientation2)
                                   (DOF1 DOF1)
                                   (DOF2 DOF2)
                                   (InterimPiece1 InterimPiece1)
                                   (InterimPiece2 InterimPiece2)
                                   (InterimPrimitive1 InterimPrimitive1)
                                   (InterimPrimitive2 InterimPrimitive2)
                                   (InterimPrimitive3 InterimPrimitive3)
                                   (DOF3 DOF3)
                                   (Orientation3 Orientation3)
                                   (DOF4 DOF4)
                                   (Orientation4 Orientation4)
                                   (DOF5 DOF5))))
  (SubGoals (($TriplePrismaticJointB  (Piece1 Piece1)
                                      (Piece2 InterimPiece1)
                                      (Primitive1 Primitive1)
                                      (Primitive2 InterimPrimitive1)
                                      (DOF1 DOF4)
                                      (DOF2 DOF2)
                                      (DOF3 DOF3)
                                      (Orientation1 Orientation3)
                                      (Orientation2 Orientation2)
                                      (Orientation3 Orientation1))
             ($CylindricalJointA (Piece1 InterimPiece2)
                                 (Piece2 Piece2)
                                 (Primitive1 InterimPrimitive2)
                                 (Primitive2 Primitive2)
                                 (Orientation Orientation1)
                                 (DOF1 DOF1)
                                 (DOF2 DOF3))))
  (Body ($NewSchemaA (Piece1 InterimPiece2)
                     (Piece2 InterimPiece1)
                     (Primitive1 InterimPrimitive2)
                     (Primitive2 InterimPrimitive3)))))
```

More General Version of $NewSchemaE

Due to pagination constraints, $NewSchemaE is split into two figures. Reproduced here are the schema's TypeSlots. The remainder of the schema can be found in Figure D.11b.

Figure D.11a

```
(TokenSlots
  (Piece1 NIL               doc (* From goalSchema))
  (Piece2 NIL               doc (* From goalSchema))
  (Primitive1 NIL           doc (* From goalSchema))
  (Primitive2 NIL           doc (* From goalSchema))
  (Orientation1 NIL         doc (* From goalSchema))
  (Orientation2 NIL         doc (* From goalSchema))
  (DOF1 NIL                 doc (* From goalSchema))
  (DOF2 NIL                 doc (* From goalSchema))
  (InterimPiece1 NIL        doc (* From goalSchema))
  (InterimPiece2 NIL        doc (* From goalSchema))
  (InterimPrimitive1 NIL    doc (* From goalSchema))
  (InterimPrimitive2 NIL    doc (* From goalSchema))
  (InterimPrimitive3 NIL    doc (* From goalSchema))
  (DOF3 NIL                 doc (* From goalSchema))
  (Orientation3 NIL         doc (* From goalSchema))
  (DOF4 NIL                 doc (* From goalSchema))
  (Orientation4 NIL         doc (* From goalSchema))
  (DOF5 NIL                 doc (* From goalSchema))
```

More General Version of $NewSchemaE, Continued

Due to pagination constraints, $NewSchemaE is split into two figures. Reproduced here are the schema's TokenSlots. The remainder of the schema can be found in Figure D.11a.

Figure D.11b

The precondition promotion cycle is used to promote certain preconditions into the new subgoal set (see Section 5.3.2.3.). In this example, all of the preconditions are promoted to the subgoal set. In addition, new slots are created (via the slot promotion process of Section 5.3.2.3) to permit the mapping of filler among the elements of the new schema.

The new schema acquired is the more operational representation of how this joint was achieved (see Figures D.12a and D.12b). It essentially states:

To achieve an instance of $SlidingRevoluteJointA, given the promoted precondition $Placed that describes the position of InterimPiece1, begin by achieving an instance of $Braced for InterimPiece1. Next achieve an $ExsertedThru of Piece1 on InterimPiece1, followed by a $BracedHoles of InterimPiece1 and Piece2. Finally, achieve a $Grasped of Interim-Piece2 and position it to achieve a $MultiAligned with InterimPiece1 and Piece2. Translate InterimPiece2 by a distance computed from the combined hole depth and the alignment offset.

Recall that the constraints on the physical characteristics of the pieces involved in this mechanism which are crucial to the success of this plan reside on the new physical joint schema $SlidingRevoluteJointA.

```
((Supers OperatorSchema)
 (TypeSlots
  (Goals (($SlidingRevoluteJointA (Piece1 Piece1)
                                  (Piece2 Piece2)
                                  (Primitive1 Primitive1)
                                  (Primitive2 Primitive2)
                                  (Orientation1 Orientation1)
                                  (Orientation2 Orientation2)
                                  (DOF1 DOF1)
                                  (DOF2 DOF2)
                                  (InterimPiece1 InterimPiece1)
                                  (InterimPiece2 InterimPiece2)
                                  (InterimPrimitive1 InterimPrimitive1)
                                  (InterimPrimitive2 InterimPrimitive2)
                                  (InterimPrimitive3 InterimPrimitive3)
                                  (DOF3 DOF3)
                                  (Orientation3 Orientation3)
                                  (DOF4 DOF4)
                                  (Orientation4 Orientation4)
                                  (DOF5 DOF5))))
   (SubGoals ((($Placed(Piece InterimPiece2)
                        (SupportSurface NewSlot2)))
             ($Braced (Piece InterimPiece1)
                      (Primitive InterimPrimitive1)
                      (Depth NewSlot3)
                      (SupportSurface NewSlot4))
             ($ExsertedThru (Piece1 Piece1)
                            (Primitive1 Primitive1)
                            (Piece2 InterimPiece1)
                            (Primitive2 InterimPrimitive1)
                            (Depth NewSlot3))
             ($BracedHoles (Piece1 Piece2)
                           (Primitive1 Primitive2)
                           (Hole1 NewSlot5)
                           (Piece2 InterimPiece1)
                           (Primitive2 InterimPrimitive3)
                           (Hole2 NewSlot6)
                           (SupportSurface2 NewSlot4)
                           (Depth NewSlot7))
                           (Piece InterimPiece2)
                           (OldSupportSurface NewSlot2)
                           (FreePrimitives InterimPrimitive2))
             ($MultiAligned (Piece1 InterimPiece2)
                            (Primitive1 InterimPrimitive2)
                            (Piece2 Piece2)
                            (Primitive2 Primitive2)
                            (Hole2 NewSlot5)
                            (Piece3 InterimPiece1)
                            (Primitive3 InterimPrimitive3)
                            (Hole3 NewSlot6)
                            (Depth NewSlot7)
                            (Delta NewSlot1)))
   (Body ($FullMove (Piece InterimPiece2)
                    (Delta NewSlot1)))))
```

More Operational Version of $NewSchemaE

Due to pagination constraints, $NewSchemaE is split into two figures. Reproduced here are the schema's TypeSlots. The remainder of the schema can be found in Figure D.12b.

Figure D.12a

```
(TokenSlots
  (Piece1 NIL                        doc (* From goalSchema))
  (Piece2 NIL                        doc (* From goalSchema))
  (Primitive1 NIL                    doc (* From goalSchema))
  (Primitive2 NIL                    doc (* From goalSchema))
  (Orientation1 NIL                  doc (* From goalSchema))
  (Orientation2 NIL                  doc (* From goalSchema))
  (DOF1 NIL                          doc (* From goalSchema))
  (DOF2 NIL                          doc (* From goalSchema))
  (InterimPiece1 NIL                 doc (* From goalSchema))
  (InterimPiece2 NIL                 doc (* From goalSchema))
  (InterimPrimitive1 NIL             doc (* From goalSchema))
  (InterimPrimitive2 NIL             doc (* From goalSchema))
  (InterimPrimitive3 NIL             doc (* From goalSchema))
  (DOF3 NIL                          doc (* From goalSchema))
  (Orientation3 NIL                  doc (* From goalSchema))
  (DOF4 NIL                          doc (* From goalSchema))
  (Orientation4 NIL                  doc (* From goalSchema))
  (DOF5 NIL                          doc (* From goalSchema))
  (NewSlot1 NIL                      doc (* Promoted slot))
  (NewSlot2 NIL                      doc (* Promoted slot))
  (NewSlot3 NIL                      doc (* Promoted slot))
  (NewSlot4 NIL                      doc (* Promoted slot))
  (NewSlot5 NIL                      doc (* Promoted slot))
  (NewSlot6 NIL                      doc (* Promoted slot))
  (NewSlot7 NIL                      doc (* Promoted slot))))
```

More Operational Version of $NewSchemaE, Continued

Due to pagination constraints, $NewSchemaE is split into two figures. Reproduced here are the schema's TokenSlots. The remainder of the schema can be found in Figure D.12a.

Figure D.12b

D.6. Solving the Same Problem After Learning

When presented with the same initial state after learning, the system produces a sequence of 19 primitive operator schemata which achieve the goal. The operator sequence is the same regardless of which version of $NewSchemaE is in use.

D.7. Solving Similar Problems After Learning

The system is capable of solving other versions of functionally similar problems. See Figure D.13 for another initial state solved by the system using either version of $NewSchemaE.

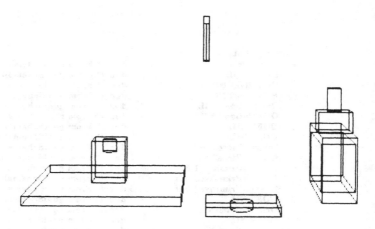

Alternate Initial State

The robot arm gripper is located in the center of the picture with its fingers closed and pointing downwards. $Frame1 is just to the left of center, and $Washer3 is in the center foreground. $Box1 is on its side at the right edge of the workspace, with $Peg4 stacked on top of it.

Figure D.13

Appendix E
Performance Considerations

In this appendix, we present some empirical results collected over several learning and problem-solving episodes [108]. These figures are intended to give a general idea of the computational resource expenditures for the sample problems in the book. For simplicity's sake, all are variants of the widget assembly of Chapter 2.

The nine examples in this appendix were collected in the order presented on a Xerox 1109 Lisp Machine running the Koto release of INTERLISP-D and the Buttress version of LOOPS. The 1109 has 3.5 megabytes of main memory, a 43 megabyte hard disk drive, and a hardware floating point coprocessor. There are several factors affecting these results that merit consideration:

(1) These results were obtained by enabling the statistics-gathering package via the $Episode::StatsFlag slot. This package greatly affects the performance of the system by (roughly) a factor of eight slowdown. Thus an episode using an hour of CPU time would actually require about seven and a half minutes without collecting statistics.

(2) All examples are run in the same 8 megabyte virtual address space. Therefore, there may be some performance degradation in the later examples due to fragmentation of the virtual address space. These effects are probably minimal.

(3) All examples are run with the graphics package ($WorkSpace:View) turned off, the causal model browser package ($Episode::Browser) turned off, and without output to a real arm ($Episode::RS232Mode). Each of these packages, when turned on, have some pejorative effect on the performance of the system.

(4)   These examples do not take advantage of the matrix operation microcode that is now available on the 1109. Matrix operations are implemented in INTERLISP-D and rely on a simple list-of-lists matrix representation. This simple representation was shown to be superior to representations based on nonlist datatypes, probably due to the high relative speed of the microcoded CDR instruction (used to extract elements from the matrix) on the 1108.

E.1. Learning Episode 1

This episode (Table E.1) corresponds to the learning episode of Chapter 2 (see Figure E.1 for starting state). The system is shown an assembly sequence of 32 primitive arm commands, and asked to generate a new operator schema. The generality/operationality tradeoff is set to generate the more operational new schema. A new physical joint schema is also generated during the verification process.

Table E.1 Learning Episode 1	
Length of observed sequence	32
Causal model size (tokens)	283
Explanation size (tokens)	242
Number of database queries	2662
Number of tokens created	8932
Number of requests issued	520883
Number of slot reads	402525
Number of slot writes	16980
Total CPU time (seconds)	7648.0
Emulator/history time (seconds)	713.2
Database time (seconds)	7416.8
Verifier (Case 3) time (seconds)	41.8
Generalizer time (seconds)	53.6

Note that the schema database uses approximately 96% of the CPU time over the length of the episode.

E.2. Problem-Solving Episode 1

This episode (Table E.2) presents the same initial state of Figure E.1 to the system for problem solving. The performance element applies the more operational new schema acquired in the learning episode described above. The assembly sequence generated has only 24 ticks,

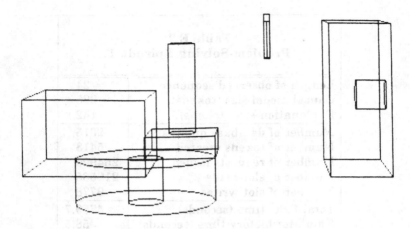

Initial State for Widget Assembly Problem

The disembodied robot arm gripper is located in the center of the picture with its fingers closed and pointing downwards. $BoredBlock1 is off to the right, with its socket also pointing to the right. $Block1 is in the left rear of the picture. $Peg1 is stacked on top of $Washer1 in the foreground, just left of center.

Figure E.1

rather than 32 as in the observed sequence. This reflects the absence of redundant commands in the sequence generated by the performance element.

The size of the planner's search tree reflects the number of nodes expanded during planning. The subtree size refers to the number of nodes actually in the plan, at all levels. The difference between these two numbers reflects the number of useless nodes expanded. As before, the database consumes well over 90% of the CPU resources.

E.3. Problem-Solving Episode 2

This problem-solving episode (Table E.3) presents the initial state shown in Figure E.2. It is a much simpler initial configuration than that of problem-solving episode 1. The planner generates a 12-element primitive arm command sequence which accomplishes the goal.

Table E.2 Problem-Solving Episode 1	
Length of observed sequence	24
Causal model size (tokens)	225
Explanation size (tokens)	142
Number of database queries	2015
Number of tokens created	5418
Number of requests issued	254906
Number of slot reads	219565
Number of slot writes	9778
Total CPU time (seconds)	4759.7
Emulator/history time (seconds)	58.5
Database time (seconds)	4471.6

As an expected side-effect of the lazy copy history mechanism, note that the average time to satisfy a database request increases with the number of layers (time ticks) in the history mechanism. In the first learning episode (32 ticks), this value was almost 3 milliseconds per request, while in this episode (12 ticks) the value is closer to 1.5 milliseconds per request.

Table E.3 Problem-Solving Episode 2	
Length of planned sequence	12
Planner search tree size (tokens)	146
Planner subtree size (tokens)	95
Number of database queries	1003
Number of tokens created	1554
Number of requests issued	84754
Number of slot reads	92593
Number of slot writes	2987
Total CPU time (seconds)	1724.5
Emulator/history time (seconds)	27.1
Database time	1560.7

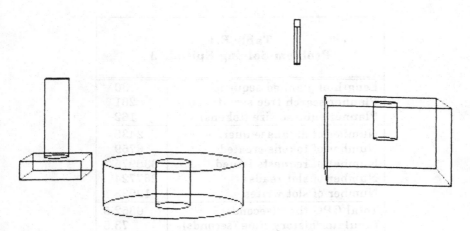

First Alternate Initial State for Widget Assembly Problem

The robot gripper is located in the center of the picture with fingers closed. $BoredBlock1 is to the right, $Peg1 is to the left, and $Washer1 is in the foreground just left of center.

Figure E.2

E.4. Problem-Solving Episode 3

This problem-solving episode (Table E.4) presents a slightly more complicated initial configuration requiring that two items be cleared off of $Washer1 during the course of the example. This is clearly reflected in the increased size of the planner subtree, which indicates the number of valid nodes expanded in planning. The initial state for this episode is shown in Figure E.3.

E.5. Problem-Solving Episode 4

This is the last problem-solving episode (Table E.5) of Chapter 2. It demonstrates the power of the system in planning the assembly of physically different yet functionally similar mechanisms. The initial state is show in Figure E.4.

Table E.4 Problem-Solving Episode 3	
Length of planned sequence	30
Planner search tree size (tokens)	261
Planner subtree size (tokens)	162
Number of database queries	2436
Number of tokens created	6759
Number of requests issued	330975
Number of slot reads	267724
Number of slot writes	12033
Total CPU time (seconds)	6352.5
Emulator/history time (seconds)	73.5
Database time (seconds)	6006.6

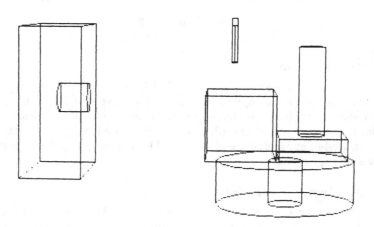

Second Alternate Initial State for Widget Assembly Problem

The robot gripper is located in the center of the picture with fingers closed. $BoredBlock1 is to the left. $Washer1 is to the right, with $Block2 and $Peg1 stacked on top of it.

Figure E.3

Table E.5 Problem-Solving Episode 4	
Length of planned sequence	18
Planner search tree size (tokens)	204
Planner subtree size (tokens)	133
Number of database queries	1753
Number of tokens created	3128
Number of requests issued	174732
Number of slot reads	184900
Number of slot writes	5433
Total CPU time (seconds)	3533.3
Emulator/history time (seconds)	47.3
Database time (seconds)	3274.2

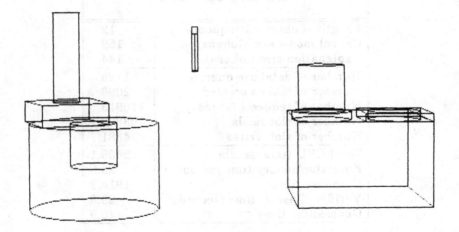

Third Alternate Initial State for Widget Assembly Problem

The robot gripper is located in the center of the picture with fingers closed. $Bored-Cylinder1 is to the left, with $Peg1 stacked on top of it. $Peg3 and $Washer2 are stacked (from left to right) on top of $Block1 on the right side of the workspace.

Figure E.4

E.6. Learning Episode 2

Clearly, it is possible to learn from a simpler initial configuration than that of Chapter 2. What kind of impact does the complexity of the observed situation have on the acquired operator schema and its subsequent performance? To address this question, we present another learning episode (Table E.6) with a much shorter solution (12 inputs as compared to the 24 of the original example). The acquired operator schema is identical, and thus its effectiveness is also identical to the originally acquired schema.

Note that the schema acquired in the first learning episode was removed from the system before running this example. However, the physical joint schema acquired in the first episode was retained: hence the verifier now recognizes the goal as a known physical joint schema (Case 2).

Table E.6 Learning Episode 2	
Length of observed sequence	12
Causal model size (tokens)	159
Explanation size (tokens)	144
Number of database queries	1129
Number of tokens created	2090
Number of requests issued	110913
Number of slot reads	103892
Number of slot writes	4581
Total CPU time (seconds)	2039.1
Emulator/history time (seconds)	23.9
Database time	1914.2
Verifier (Case 2) time (seconds)	29.8
Generalizer time	40.9

E.7. Learning Episode 3

Perhaps the most interesting aspect of these results are their bearing on the generality/operationality tradeoff discussed in Section 5.3.2.3. To investigate this in empirical terms, we present another observation episode (Table E.7), identical to the simpler initial configuration of the previous example (see Figure E.1). This time the system generates the more general new operator schema.

The new schema acquired in the previous episode was, of course, removed from the system before presenting this example. As before, however, the physical joint schema acquired in the first episode was retained, allowing the verifier to operate under Case 2.

As expected, the results shown here are almost identical to the results of the previous, identical, episode. The only difference is in the time spent on generalization. The extra analysis required to produce the more operational new schema is clearly evident in the greater CPU time figure in the operational case. This is consistent with expected behavior.

Table E.7 Learning Episode 3	
Length of observed sequence	12
Causal model size (tokens)	159
Explanation size (tokesn)	144
Number of database queries	1117
Number of tokens created	2072
Number of requests issued	109639
Number of slot reads	102380
Number of slot writes	4573
Total CPU time (seconds)	2047.8
Emulator/history time (seconds)	24.6
Database time (seconds)	1935.0
Verifier (Case 2) time (seconds)	31.7
Generalizer time (seconds)	26.4

E.8. Problem-Solving Episode 5

This example is identical to problem-solving episode (Table E.8) 2 (see Figure E.2), except that the new schema being applied is the more general version. We therefore expect this example to be less efficient, since the planner must work harder when applying a more general schema.

The expected behavior is evident in the total CPU time figure (42 minutes as compared to 29 minutes in the other case). In addition, the planner subtree is a bit larger: but since the additional nodes tend to be at the highest level of abstraction, the increase in CPU time tends to be more than linear in the increased subtree size.

E.9. Problem-Solving Episode 6

Episode 6 (Table E.9) is identical to problem-solving episode 4 (see Figure E.4). Since it represents the most complicated of the four examples from Chapter 2, it was chosen to complement the simple example of problem-solving episode 5.

These results are consistent with expected behavior.

Table E.8
Problem-Solving Episode 5

Length of planned sequence	12
Planner search tree size (tokens)	151
Planner subtree size (tokens)	138
Number of database queries	1340
Number of tokens created	2044
Number of requests issued	118962
Number of slot reads	139695
Number of slot writes	3661
Total CPU time (seconds)	2498.8
Emulator/history time (seconds)	25.8
Database time (seconds)	2219.3

Table E.9
Problem-Solving Episode 6

Length of planned sequence	18
Planner search tree size (tokens)	215
Planner subtree size (tokesn)	194
Number of database queries	2357
Number of tokens created	3952
Number of requests issued	256358
Number of slot reads	287017
Number of slot writes	3427
Total CPU time (seconds)	5257.7
Emulator/history time (seconds)	45.4
Database time (seconds)	4861.8

Appendix F
Built-In Schemata

In this appendix, we present a capsule summary of each schema initially built into the ARMS schema library.

F.1. State Schemata

$Aligned

A planar surface on a piece is parallel to and facing a hole on another piece which is the object of a $BracedHole.

$AlignedHole

Similar to $Aligned, but refers to a hole aligned with a surface which is the object of a $Braced.

$AlignedHoles

Similar to $Aligned, but refers to a second hole aligned with the object of the $BracedHole.

$At

Describes the position of the robot gripper.

$Braced

Establishes that a planar surface on a given piece is parallel with the workspace surface, i.e., pointing up.

$BracedHole

Same as $Braced, but describes a hole on the piece.

$BracedHoles

Similar to $BracedHole, but describes two holes from two different pieces which are aligned and both pointing up. The upper piece's hole must go all the way through to the lower piece's hole.

$Cleared

Establishes that a given piece has no other piece on top of it.

$Closed

States the gripper is closed.

$Downturned

Establishes that a planar surface on a given piece is parallel with the workspace surface, but (as opposed to $Braced) is pointing down.

$DownturnedHole

Similar to $Downturned, but describes a hole.

$Empty

The gripper is empty.

$Exserted

A negative primitive from one piece is used to surround a primitive from another piece. The dual of $Inserted.

$ExsertedThru

Similar to $Exserted, but the insertion goes all the way through the piece.

$Facing

The gripper is poiting towards a surface of a piece. This is usually preperatory to approaching the piece and grasping it.

$Grasped

The gripper is holding a piece.

$Inserted

A primitive from one piece is inserted into a negative primitive from another piece.

$InsertedThru

Similar to $Inserted, but the insertion goes all the way through the piece.

$MultiAligned

A primitive from one piece is aligned with two holes described by a $BracedHoles.

$Opened

The gripper is opened.

$Placed

Describes the position of a piece not held by the gripper.

$Positioned

Describes the position of a piece while held by the gripper.

$Stacked

Describes a support relation between two pieces.

$Surrounds

Describes the state where the gripper, fingers opened, surrounds a piece.

$UnHindered

Describes the state where there is nothing between the

opened fingers of the gripper.

F.1.1. Joint Schemata

$CylindricalJoint
　　Abstract joint schema with a revolute and a prismatic degree of freedom on the same axis.

$CylindricalJointA
　　Physical joint schema achieved by inserting a cylindrical primitive into a slightly larger hole.

$CylindricalJointB
　　Same as $CylindricalJointA, but with arguments reversed.

$RevoluteJoint
　　Abstract joint schema with a single revolute degree of freedom.

$RigidJoint
　　Abstract joint schema with no degrees of freedom.

$RigidJointA
　　Physical joint schema achieved by inserting a primitive into a hole of the same dimension.

$RigidJointB
　　Same as $RigidJointA, but with arguments reversed.

$SlidingRevoluteJoint
　　Abstract joint schema with a revolute and a prismatic degree of freedom on orthogonal axes.

$TriplePrismaticJoint
　　Abstract joint schema with three prismatic degrees of freedom.

$TriplePrismaticJointA
　　Physical joint schema achieved by inserting a square primitive into a square socket.

$TriplePrismaticJointB
　　Same as $TriplePrismaticJointA, but with arguments reversed.

F.1.2. Degree of Freedom Schemata

$PrismaticDOF
　　Describes a prismatic degree of freedom. See section 6.5.2.2.1.1.

$RevoluteDOF
　　Describes a revolute degree of freedom. See section 6.5.2.2.1.1.

F.1.3. Constraint Schemata

$ConstraintSchema
>   All constraints are tokens of this type. See section 6.5.2.1.

F.2. Operator Schemata

$Align
>   Operator schema for achieving $Aligned.

$AlignHole
>   Operator schema for achieving $AlignedHole.

$AlignHoles
>   Operator schema for achieving $AlignedHoles.

$Approach
>   Operator schema for achieving $Surrounds.

$Brace
>   Operator schema for achieving $Braced.

$BraceHole
>   Operator schema for achieving $BracedHole.

$BraceHoles
>   Operator schema for achieving $BracedHoles.

$Disengage
>   Operator schema for achieving $UnHindered.

$Downturn
>   Operator schema for achieving $Downturned.

$DownturnHole
>   Operator schema for achieving $DownturnedHole.

$Drop
>   Operator schema for achieving $Empty.

$EmptyMove
>   Operator schema for achieving $At.

$Exsert
>   Operator schema for achieving $Exserted.

$ExsertThru
>   Operator schema for achieving $ExsertedThru.

$Face
>   Operator schema for achieving $Facing.

$FullMove
>   Operator schema for achieving $Positioned.

$Insert
>   Operator schema for achieving $Inserted.

$InsertThru
>   Operator schema for achieving $InsertedThru.

$MultiAlign
    Operator schema for achieving $MultiAligned.
$Pickup
    Operator schema for achieving $Grasped.
$Place
    Operator schema for achieving $Placed.
$Stack
    Operator schema for achieving $Stacked.
$UnStack
    Operator schema for defeating $Stacked.

F.2.1. Primitive Operator Schemata

$Close
    Operator schema executed by robot arm to achieve $Closed.
$MoveTo
    Operator schema executed by robot arm to achieve $At.
$Open
    Operator schema executed by robot arm to achieve $Opened.
$Rotate
    Operator schema executed by robot arm to achieve $At.
$Translate
    Operator schema executed by robot arm to achieve $At.

References

1. G. D. Ritchie and F. K. Hanna, "AM: A Case Study in Artificial Intelligence Methodology", *Artificial Intelligence 23* (1984), 249-268.

2. G. F. DeJong, "Generalizations Based on Explanations", *Proceedings of the Seventh International Joint Conference on Artificial Intelligence*, Vancouver, B.C., Canada, August 1981, 67-69.

3. G. F. DeJong, "Acquiring Schemata through Understanding and Generalizing Plans", *Proceedings of the Eighth International Joint Conference on Artificial Intelligence*, Karlsruhe, West Germany, August 1983, 462-464.

4. T. M. Mitchell, R. Keller and S. Kedar-Cabelli, "Explanation-Based Generalization: A Unifying View", *Machine Learning 1*, 1 (January 1986), 47-80.

5. G. F. DeJong and R. J. Mooney, "Explanation-Based Learning: An Alternative View", *Machine Learning 1*, 2 (April 1986).

6. G. F. DeJong, "Explanation Based Learning", in *Machine Learning: An Artificial Intelligence Approach, Vol. II*, Morgan Kaufmann, Los Altos, CA, 1986.

7. A. Bundy, "Some Suggested Criteria for Assessing Artificial Intelligence Research", *Workshop on the Foundations of Artificial Intelligence*, Las Cruces, NM, February 1986, 46-48.

8. D. McDermott, "Artificial Intelligence Meets Natural Stupidity", *SIGART Newsletter 57* (April 1976), 4-9.

9.   J. McCarthy, "Programs with Common Sense", *Proceedings of the Symposium on the Mechanization of Thought Processes, National Physical Laboratory*, Teddington, England, 1958, 77-84.

10.   A. M. Segre and R. Schank, "The Current State of Artificial Intelligence: One Man's Opinion", *Artificial Intelligence Magazine 4*, 1 (Winter/Spring 1983), 3-8, Kluwer Academic Publishers.

11.   B. C. Smith, "Reflection and Semantics in a Procedural Language", Ph.D. Thesis, Department of Computer Science, MIT, Cambridge, MA, 1982.

12.   H. Simon, "Why Should Machines Learn?", in *Machine Learning: An Artificial Intelligence Approach*, Tioga Publishing Company, Palo Alto, CA, 1983, 24-37.

13.   T. Lozano-Perez, "Robot Programming", Memo 698, Artificial Intelligence Laboratory, Massachusetts Institute of Technology, Cambridge, MA, December 1982.

14.   R. H. Taylor, P. D. Summers and J. M. Meyer, "AML: A Manufacturing Language", *International Journal of Robotics Research 1*, 3 (Fall 1982), 19-41.

15.   A. M. Segre, "Explanation-Based Learning of Generalized Robot Assembly Plans", Ph.D. Thesis, Department of Electrical and Computer Engineering, University of Illinois at Urbana-Champaign, Urbana, IL, January 1987.

16.   R. S. Michalski, "A Theory and Methodology of Inductive Learning", in *Machine Learning: An Artificial Intelligence Approach*, Tioga Publishing Company, Palo Alto, CA, 1983, 83-134.

17.   E. Shortliffe, *Computer Based Medical Consultations: MYCIN*, American Elsevier, NY, 1976.

18.   R. S. Michalski and R. L. Chilausky, "Learning by Being Told and Learning from Examples: An Experimental Comparison of the Two Methods of Knowledge Acquisition in the Context of Developing an Expert System for Soybean Disease Diagnosis", *Policy Analysis and Information Systems 4*, 2 (June 1980), 125-160.

19.   R. E. Stepp, Personal Communication, June 1986.

20.   R. E. Stepp, "Conjunctive Conceptual Clustering: A Methodology and Experimentation", Ph.D. Thesis, Department of Computer Science, University of Illinois at Urbana-Champaign, Urbana, IL, 1984.

21.   L. Rendell, "A General Framework for Induction and a Study of Selective Induction", *Machine Learning 1*, 2 (1986), 177-226.

22. S. A. Rajamoney, "Automated Design of Experiments for Refining Theories", M. S. Thesis, Department of Computer Science, UI, Urbana, IL, May 1986.

23. T. Mitchell, "Learning and Problem Solving", *Proceedings of the Eighth International Joint Conference on Artificial Intelligence*, Karlsruhe, West Germany, August 1983, 1139-1151.

24. T. M. Mitchell, "Version Spaces: An Approach to Concept Learning", Technical Report STAN-CS-78-711, Stanford University, Palo Alto, CA, 1978.

25. R. E. Fikes, P. E. Hart and N. J. Nilsson, "Learning and Executing Generalized Robot Plans", *Artificial Intelligence 3* (1972), 251-288.

26. T. Mitchell, S. Mahadevan and L. Steinberg, "A Learning Apprentice System for VLSI Design", *Proceedings of the 1985 International Machine Learning Workshop*, Skytop, PA, June 1985, 123-125.

27. B. Silver, "Using Meta-level Inference to Constrain Search and to Learn Strategies in Equation Solving", Ph.D. Thesis, Department of Artificial Intelligence, University of Edinburgh, 1984.

28. P. V. O'Rorke, "Generalization for Explanation-based Schema Acquisition", *Proceedings of the National Conference on Artificial Intelligence*, Austin, TX, August 1984, 260-263.

29. P. V. O'Rorke, "LT Revisited: Experimental Results of Applying Explanation-Based Learning to the Logic of Principia Matematica", *Proceedings of the 1987 International Machine Learning Workshop*, Irvine, CA, June 1987, 148-159.

30. J. W. Shavlik, "Learning about Momentum Conservation", *Proceedings of the Ninth International Joint Conference on Artificial Intelligence*, Los Angeles, CA, August 1985, 667-669.

31. J. W. Shavlik and G. F. DeJong, "Building a Computer Model of Learning Classical Mechanics", *Proceedings of the Seventh Annual Conference of the Cognitive Science Society*, Irvine, CA, August 1985, 351-355.

32. R. J. Mooney and G. F. DeJong, "Learning Schemata for Natural Language Processing", *Proceedings of the Ninth International Joint Conference on Artificial Intelligence*, Los Angeles, CA, August 1985, 681-687.

33. D. Gentner, "Structure-Mapping: A Theoretical Framework for Analogy", *Cognitive Science 7*, 2 (1983), 155-170.

34. K. D. Forbus, "Qualitative Process Theory", Technical Report 789, Ph.D. Thesis, Artificial Intelligence Laboratory, Massachusetts Institute of Technology, Cambridge, MA, August 1984.

35. P. J. Hayes, "The Naive Physics Manifesto", in *Expert Systems in the Micro-Electronic Age*, Edinburgh University Press, Edinburgh, Scotland, 1979, 242-270.

36. W. Chafe, "Some Thoughts on Schemata", *Theoretical Issues in Natural Language Processing 1*, Cambridge, MA, 1975, 89-91.

37. M. L. Minsky, "A Framework for Representing Knowledge", in *The Psychology of Computer Vision*, McGraw-Hill, New York, NY, 1975, 211-277.

38. E. Charniak, "On the Use of Framed Knowledge in Language Comprehension", *Artificial Intelligence 11*, 3 (1978), 225-265.

39. R. C. Schank and R. P. Abelson, *Scripts, Plans, Goals and Understanding: An Inquiry into Human Knowledge Structures*, Lawrence Erlbaum and Associates, Hillsdale, NJ, 1977.

40. S. E. Fahlman, *NETL: A System for Representing and Using Real-World Knowledge*, MIT Press, Cambridge, MA, 1979.

41. G. F. DeJong, "Skimming Stories in Real Time: An Experiment in Integrated Understanding", Technical Report 158, Ph.D. Thesis, Department of Computer Science, Yale University, New Haven, CT, 1979.

42. E. Charniak, "With a Spoon in Hand this Must be the Eating Frame", *Theoretical Issues in Natural Language Processing 2*, Urbana, IL, 1978, 187-193.

43. B. Gustafson, "Development of Localized Planner for Artificial Intelligence-Based Robot Task Planning System", M.S. Thesis, University of Illinois at Urbana-Champaign, Urbana, IL, October 1986.

44. V. Hayward and R. Paul, "Introduction to RCCL: A Robot Control 'C' Library", *Proceedings of the IEEE International Conference on Robotics and Automation*, Atlanta, GA, 1984, 293-297.

45. S. M. Udupa, "Collision Detection and Avoidance in Computer Controller Manipulators", *Proceedings of the Fifth International Joint Conference on Artificial Intelligence*, Cambridge, MA, August 1977.

46. T. Lozano-Perez and M. Wesley, "An Algorithm for Planning Collision-Free Paths Among Polyhedral Obstacles", *Communications of the Association for Computing Machinery 22*, 10

(October 1979), 560-570.

47. R. Tilove, "Extending Solid Modeling Systems for Mechanism Design and Kinematic Simulation", *IEEE Computer Graphics and Applications 3*, 3 (May 1983), 9-19.

48. BBN, *Butterfly Parallel Processor Overview, Version 1*, Bolt, Baranek and Newmann, Inc., Cambridge, MA, 1985.

49. C. Seitz, "The Cosmic Cube", *Communications of the Association for Computing Machinery 28*, 1 (January 1985), 22-33.

50. P. E. Friedland, "Knowledge-based Experiment Design in Molecular Genetics", Technical Report 79-771, Computer Science Department, Stanford University, Palo Alto, CA, 1979.

51. E. Charniak, "MS. MALAPROP, A Language Comprehension System", *Proceedings of the Fifth International Joint Conference on Artificial Intelligence*, Cambridge, MA, August 1977.

52. G. F. DeJong, "Prediction and Substantiation: A New Approach for Natural Language Processing", *Cognitive Science 3*, 3 (1980), 251-273.

53. R. W. Wilensky, "Understanding Goal-Based Stories", Technical Report 140, Ph.D. Thesis, Department of Computer Science, Yale University, New Haven, CT, September 1978.

54. R. E. Cullingford, "Script Application: Computer Understanding of Newspaper Stories", Technical Report 116, Department of Computer Science, Yale University, New Haven, CT, January 1978.

55. E. Charniak, "Context Recognition in Language Comprehension", in *Strategies for Natural Language Processing*, Lawrence Erlbaum and Associates, Hillsdale, NJ , 1982, 435-454.

56. D. G. Bobrow and M. Stefik, *LOOPS Reference Manual*, Xerox PARC, Palo Alto, CA, 1983.

57. W. Teitelman, *Interlisp Reference Manual*, Xerox PARC, Palo Alto, CA, 1983.

58. J. G. Schmolze and R. J. Brachman (ed.), "Proceedings of the 1981 KL-One Workshop", Technical Report 4842, Bolt, Baranek and Newmann, Inc., Cambridge, MA, June 1982.

59. R. Brachman, R. E. Fikes and H. Levesque, "KRYPTON: A Functional Approach to Knowledge Representation", in *Readings in Knowledge Representation*, Morgan Kaufmann, Los Altos, CA, 1985, 411-430.

60. D. G. Bobrow and T. W. Winograd, "An Overview of KRL, A Knowledge Representation Language", *Cognitive Science 1* (1977), 3-46.

61. B. R. Roberts and I. P. Goldstein, "The FRL Manual", Memo 409, Artificial Intelligence Laboratory, Massachusetts Institute of Technology, Cambridge, MA, September 1977.

62. E. Charniak, M. Gavin and J. Hendler, "The Frail/Nasl Reference Manual", Technical Report CS-83-06, Brown University Department of Computer Science, Providence, RI, February 1983.

63. W. Newman and R. Sproull, *Principles of Interactive Computer Graphics*, McGraw-Hill, New York, NY, 1973.

64. G. F. DeJong, R. J. Mooney, S. A. Rajamoney, A. M. Segre and J. W. Shavlik, "A Review of Explanation-Based Learning", Technical Report, Artificial Intelligence Research Group, Coordinated Science Laboratory, University of Illinois at Urbana-Champaign, Urbana, IL, 1987.

65. T. M. Mitchell, S. Mahadevan and L. I. Steinberg, "LEAP: A Learning Apprentice for VLSI Design", *Proceedings of the Ninth International Joint Conference on Artificial Intelligence*, Los Angeles, CA, August 1985, 573-580.

66. R. J. Mooney and S. W. Bennett, "A Domain Independent Explanation-Based Generalizer", *Proceedings of the National Conference on Artificial Intelligence*, Philadelphia, PA, August 1986, 551-555.

67. K. Hammond, "CHEF: A Model of Case-Based Planning", *Proceedings of the National Conference on Artificial Intelligence*, Philadelphia, PA, August 1986, 267-271.

68. P. Rosenbloom and J. Laird, "Mapping Explanation-Based Generalization into Soar", *Proceedings of the National Conference on Artificial Intelligence*, Philadelphia, PA, August 1986, 561-567.

69. M. Pazzani, M. Dyer and M. Flowers, "The Role of Prior Causal Theories in Generalization", *Proceedings of the National Conference on Artificial Intelligence*, Philadelphia, PA, August 1986, 545-550.

70. M. Lebowitz, "Complex Learning Environments: Hierarchies and the Use of Explanation", in *Machine Learning: A Guide To Current Research*, Kluwer Academic Publishers, Hingham, MA, 1986, 179-182.

71. P. R. Cohen and E. A. Feigenbaum, *The Handbook of Artificial Intelligence, Volume III*, William Kaufman, Inc., Los Altos, CA, 1982.

72. R. Reiter, "On Reasoning by Default", *Theoretical Issues in Natural Language Processing 2*, Urbana, IL, July 1978, 210-218.

73. A. Newell, J. C. Shaw and H. A. Simon, "Empirical Explorations with the Logic Theory Machine: A Case Study in Heuristics", in *Computers and Thought*, McGraw-Hill, New York, NY, 1963.

74. T. M. Mitchell, L. Steinberg and J. Shulman, "A Knowledge-Based Approach to Design", Technical Report LCSR-TR-65, Rutgers University, New Brunswick, NJ , January 1985.

75. D. C. Wilkins, W. J. Clancey and B. G. Buchanan, "ODYSSEUS: A Learning Apprentice", in *Machine Learning: A Guide To Current Research*, Kluwer Academic Publishers, Hingham, MA, 1986, 369-374.

76. W. Clancey and R. Letsinger, "NEOMYCIN: Reconfiguring a Rule-Based Expert System for Application to Teaching", in *Proceedings of the Seventh International Joint Conference on Artificial Intelligence*, Vancouver, B.C., Canada, August 1981, 829-836.

77. S. N. Minton, "Overview of the PRODIGY Learning Apprentice", in *Machine Learning: A Guide To Current Research*, Kluwer Academic Publishers, Hingham, MA, 1986, 199-202.

78. S. Fahlman, "A Planning System for Robot Construction Tasks", *Artificial Intelligence 5* (1974), 1-49.

79. C. Brown, "PADL-2: A Technical Summary", *IEEE Computer Graphics and Applications 2*, 2 (March 1982), 69-84.

80. J. Boyse and J. Gilchrist, "GMSOLID - Interactive Modeling for Design and Analysis of Solids", Technical Report GMR-3882, GM Research Laboratories, Warren, MI, November 1981.

81. P. Veenman, "ROMULUS - The Design of a Geometric Modeller", Technical Report P-80-GM-01, CAM-I, Inc., Bournemouth, U.K., November 1979.

82. J. de Kleer, "An Assumption-based TMS", *Artificial Intelligence 28*, 2 (March 1986), 127-162.

83. J. de Kleer, "Problem Solving with the ATMS", *Artificial Intelligence 28*, 2 (March 1986), 197-224.

84. D. A. McAllester, "An Outlook on Truth Maintenance", Memo 551, Artificial Intelligence Laboratory, Massachusetts Institute of Technology, Cambridge, MA, August 1980.

85. D. A. McAllester, "Reasoning Utility Package User's Manual, Version One", Memo 667, Artificial Intelligence Laboratory, Massachusetts Institute of Technology, Cambridge, MA, April

1982.

86. J. Doyle, "Truth Maintenance Systems for Problem Solving", Technical Report 419, Artificial Intelligence Laboratory, Massachusetts Institute of Technology, Cambridge, MA, 1978.

87. R. Michalski, "Understanding the Nature of Learning: Issues and Research Directions", in *Machine Learning: An Artificial Intelligence Approach, Vol. II*, Morgan Kaufmann, Los Altos, CA, 1986, 3-25.

88. J. F. Allen, "Maintaining Knowledge about Temporal Intervals", *Communications of the Association for Computing Machinery 26*, 11 (November 1983), 832-843.

89. T. Dean, "Time Map Maintenance", Technical Report 289, Department of Computer Science, Yale University, New Haven, CT, October 1983.

90. D. McDermott, "A Temporal Logic for Reasoning About Processes and Plans", *Cognitive Science 6*, 2 (1982), 101-155.

91. A. E. Prieditis, "Discovery of Algorithms from Weak Methods", *Proceedings of the International Meeting on Advances in Learning*, Les Arcs, Switzerland, 1986, 37-52.

92. P. W. Cheng and J. G. Carbonell, "The FERMI System: Inducing Iterative Macro-operators from Experience", *Proceedings of the National Conference on Artificial Intelligence*, Philadelphia, PA, August 1986, 490-495.

93. R. J. Doyle, "Constructing and Refining Causal Explanations from an Inconsistent Domain Theory", *Proceedings of the National Conference on Artificial Intelligence*, Philadelphia, PA, August 1986, 538-544.

94. R. A. Brooks, "Symbolic Error Analysis and Robot Planning", Memo 685, Artificial Intelligence Laboratory, Massachusetts Institute of Technology, Cambridge, MA, September 1982.

95. T. Lozano-Perez, M. Mason and R. Taylor, "Automatic Synthesis of Fine-Motion Strategies for Robots", *International Journal of Robotics Research 3*, 1 (1984), 3-24.

96. M. Gini and G. Gini, "Towards Automatic Error Recovery in Robot Programs", *Proceedings of the Eighth International Joint Conference on Artificial Intelligence*, Karlsruhe, West Germany, August 1983, 821-823.

97. D. Wilkins, "Domain-Independant Planning: Representation and Plan Generation", *Artificial Intelligence 22* (April 1984), 269-301.

98. D. Wilkins, "Monitoring the Execution of Plans in SIPE", Technical Report, SRI International, Menlo Park, CA, September 1984.

99. A. A. G. Requicha and H. B. Voelcker, "Solid Modeling: A Historical Summary and Contemporary Assessment", *IEEE Computer Graphics and Applications 2*, 2 (March 1982), 9-24.

100. A. A. G. Requicha and H. B. Voelcker, "Solid Modeling: Current Status and Research Directions", *IEEE Computer Graphics and Applications 3*, 5 (October 1983), 25-37.

101. I. Braid, "The Synthesis of Solids Bound by Many Faces", *Communications of the Association for Computing Machinery 18*, 4 (April 1975), 209-216.

102. R. Hillyard, "The Build Group of Solid Modelers", *IEEE Computer Graphics and Applications 2*, 2 (March 1982), 43-52.

103. H. B. Voelcker, "The PADL-1.0/2 System for Defining and Displaying Solid Objects", *Computer Graphics 12*, 3 (August 1978), 257-263.

104. A. A. G. Requicha, "Representations for Rigid Solids", *Association for Computing Machinery Computing Surveys 12*, 4 (December 1980), 437-464.

105. W. Gordon, "An Operator Calculus for Surface and Volume Modeling", *IEEE Computer Graphics and Applications 3*, 5 (October 1983), 18-22.

106. R. Sarraga, "Computation of Surface Areas in GMSOLID", Technical Report GMR-4036, GM Research Laboratories, Warren, MI, April 1982.

107. R. Sarraga and W. Waters, "Free-Form Surfaces in GMSOLID: Goals and Issues", Technical Report GMR-4481, GM Research Laboratories, Warren, MI, September 1983.

108. A. M. Segre, "On the Operationality/Generality Trade-Off in Explanation-Based Learning", *Proceedings of the Tenth International Joint Conference on Artificial Intelligence*, Milan, Italy, August 1987, 242-248.

Index